Garland Studies in _____

COMPARATIVE
LITERATURE ___

GENERAL EDITOR
James J. Wilhelm
Rutgers University

ASSOCIATE EDITOR
Richard Saez
College of Staten Island, C.U.N.Y.

A GARLAND SERIES

NATIONAL HISTORY_
IN THE HEROIC POEM
A COMPARISON OF THE *AENEID*
AND *THE FAERIE QUEENE*

Nancy P. Pope

GARLAND PUBLISHING
New York & London
1990

Library of Congress Cataloging-in-Publication Data

Pope, Nancy P. (Nancy Patricia)
National history in the heroic poem: a comparison of the Aeneid
and the Faerie queene/ Nancy P. Pope.
p. cm.—(Garland studies in comparative literature)
Thesis (Ph. D.)—Washington University, 1982.
Includes bibliographical references.
ISBN 0-8240-5472-5 (alk. paper)
1. Virgil, Aeneis. 2. Virgil—Knowledge—History. 3. Spenser, Edmund,
1552?–1599. Faerie queene. 4. Spenser, Edmund, 1552?–1599—Knowledge—History. 5. Arthurian romances—Adaptions—History and criticism.
6. Aeneas (Legendary character) in literature. 7. Literature, Comparative—
Latin and English. 8. Literature, Comparative—English and Latin.
9. Historical poetry—History and criticism. 10. Epic poetry—History and
criticism. 11. Great Britain in literature. 12. Rome in literature
I. Title. II. Series.
PA6825.P57   1990
809.1'32—dc20   90-42002

Printed on acid-free, 250-year-life paper.
Manufactured in the United States of America

This dissertation is dedicated
to my husband, Michael Thomas,
without whom it would not exist.

TABLE OF CONTENTS

ACKNOWLEDGEMENTS

This dissertation came into existence with the aid of the best possible advisory committee. Professors Revard, Matheson, and Herbert have been supportive, painstaking, and immensely helpful. I am particularly indebted to Kevin Herbert for his advice on the Aeneid, Carter Revard for his advice on The Faerie Queene, and William Matheson for his advice on the style of my text and my translations. I am also grateful for the more recent aid of Professor Joseph Loewenstein in updating the bibliography. Any remaining faults are, of course, solely mine.

The schools which employ me, Washington University and Webster University, have been generous in giving me access to materials and time to revise my dissertation for publication. My children have also been unusually patient about my physical absences and frequent absentmindedness during the revision process. Finally, I would like to thank Doris Suits for her excellent typing, both in 1982 and again in 1990; Margret Brown for repeatedly making a departmental computer available to me; and my editor, Dr. J. Scott Bentley, for his steadfast interest and encouragement.

This dissertation examines the ways in which Spenser's use of British history in The Faerie Queene imitates and transforms Vergil's use of Roman history in the Aeneid. The first two chapters analyze the forms, themes, and narrative functions of Anchises' prophecy (Aeneid VI) and Merlin's prophecy (Faerie Queene III), with particular attention to the role the prophecies play in committing Aeneas and Britomart to their destined tasks. The third and fourth chapters provide similar analyses of Aeneas' visit to the site of Rome and the shield he receives (Aeneid VIII) and of Arthur's visit to the castle of Alma and the chronicle he reads (Faerie Queene II), with particular attention to the political and moral examples set before the heroes. The fifth chapter considers the use of history in Ariosto's Orlando Furioso and Tasso's Gerusalemme Liberata, works from which Spenser frequently borrowed and which themselves imitated the Aeneid. I show that Ariosto and Tasso could not have furnished Spenser with either the themes or the narrative functions which his historical passages share with Vergil's. Therefore, I conclude, Spenser modelled his use of national history in a heroic poem on Vergil's.

My dissertation has gained allies and, in the process, lost some of the uniqueness from my not publishing it until now. I made three major points about the Aeneid: Vergil's praise of Rome and Augustus should be taken at face value; Aeneas is a fictional personage who makes mistakes and has human emotions; and the lessons Evander teaches Aeneas parallel those the shield teaches the reader. Most pre-World War II critics

accepted Vergil's patriotism, which became objectionable in the 1960s
and '70s, just as consideration of Aeneas' humanity began. Many current
critics share my interpretations of praise and of character in the
Aeneid, but no one else has noticed the parallels I find in Book VIII.
Similarly, I made three major points about The Faerie Queene: Arthur and
Britomart are fictional personages, rather than personifications, and are
affected by the chronicle cantos (II.x and III.iii); the lessons Arthur
learns from the chronicle he reads parallel those the readers learn from
the castle he visits; and Spenser deliberately imitated Vergil in his
historical passages. The first point now has other adherents, but no
one else fully agrees with the second or has noticed the third. The
remainder of this preface discusses the relation of my dissertation to
these critical trends.[1]

In the 1960s and '70s, patriotism and heroism underwent significant
changes in this country. Using civil disobedience to protest American
involvement in the war in Vietnam was widely considered more patriotic
than obeying the American government, and refusing to fight was similarly considered more heroic than fighting. Many classicists of the
so-called "Harvard school" projected these modern values on Vergil. My
disagreement with their interpretation of the Aeneid produced most of the
notes to Chapters 2 and 3. Although this school of criticism still
flourishes,[2] the trend has been toward a synthesis, recognizing a mixture
of positive and negative feelings both in the text and in the reader's
responses. Not surprisingly, the mixture differs from critic to critic.
For example, Gotoff finds Anchises' prophecy ambivalent and the shield
positive, whereas Griffin finds the prophecy ambivalent and the shield

negative. Hardie uses a wholly different approach to the shield from
mine, yet we reach very similar--and very positive--conclusions.

In addition to interpreting Books VI and VIII positively, I argue
that both books cause Aeneas to change. Before the Harvard school
became influential, most classicists described pius Aeneas as a figure
with no feelings, one epithet, and at most two dimensions. More careful
attention to the text in the 1960s and '70s uncovered many indications of
emotion, error, and alteration in Aeneas. Today, critics with sharply
divergent interpretations of the Aeneid agree on its hero's humanity,
sometimes arriving independently at my understanding of his character
and its development. Burnell uses a variety of Roman sources to prove
that Aeneas behaves badly in Book II, a judgment I use completely different evidence to support. Quint's article on memories of the past in
Book II coincides with my discussion of that theme in most particulars,
although his general assessment of Vergil's attitude toward Roman politics
is more negative. Mack's analysis of prophecies of the immediate future
in Books I-VIII (56-67) comes very close to mine, though her reading of
prophecies of the distant future in Books I, VI, and VIII (67-75) is
radically different. These three works collectively agree with my
discussion of Books I-V, while either ignoring Book VI or arguing against
my interpretation of it.[3]

Finally, I found parallels between the lessons Aeneas learns from
Evander and those shown on the shield. Since Aeneas does not understand
his shield's engraving, most critics assume that he has not learned the
lessons it teaches. Yet most of them agree that the Hercules episode
and the site of Rome offer moral instruction; Harrison's and Yardley's

articles explain two of Book VIII's teachings. If, as I argue, these
explicit forms of instruction teach the same lessons as the more enigmatic
shield, then Aeneas does end Book VIII in possession of both understanding
and armor. This point is not made by any of the other critics in the
1980s.

In _The Faerie Queene_, as in the _Aeneid_, my argument that the historical passages cause characters to change depends on the assumption that
these characters are fictional personages, capable of changing. Most
earlier Spenserians assumed that his characters had immutable allegorical
significance instead of mutable human nature. In the 1960s and '70s,
however, valuable distinctions among Spenser's characters began to appear.
While critics do not yet agree about many of the secondary figures, they
generally accept the British knights as fictional human beings who
gradually attain their respective virtues rather than constantly personi-
fying them. Britomart has greatly benefited from this new attitude. For
example, Cheney's and Wofford's articles argue that she changes in the
course of Book III, although neither one attributes her alteration to
Merlin's prophecy. Deneef agrees with me that both Glauce and Merlin
correct Britomart's attitude toward her own passions (162-63). Broaddus
finds thematic connections between Merlin's prophecy and the psychological
allegory of Book III, without considering the effect of the prophecy on
Britomart's psyche. In short, these four critics interpret the historical
material in III.iii and/or its narrative context as I do, but they do not
see the relation I see between that material and the character who hears
it.

My argument about the relation between the chronicle in II.x and

its narrative context has two parts: that the chronicle's political
lessons parallel Alma's moral lessons in the preceding canto and that
reading the chronicle enables Arthur to defeat Maleger in the following
canto. Wells (61-62) and Rossi (57-58) note that the chronicle's
beleaguered Britain parallels Alma's besieged castle. Moreover, Rossi's
interpretation of the chronicle almost duplicates mine, especially in
showing that its political lessons are identical to Book II's moral
lessons. Rollinson comes to the same conclusions as I do about Maleger's
representing misrule (106-08), although he develops the concept only in
moral terms. Taken together, these three critics find most of the
parallels that I find between II.x and its context, but they do not see
the relation I see between the chronicle and the character who reads it.

Finally, throughout my dissertation I argue that Spenser imitated
Vergil's use of historical material. The 1980s saw a great renewal of
interest in the theory and practice of imitation; even critics who focus
on a single text often glance at earlier or later texts in passing, far
more than was common ten years ago.[4] Among the Vergilians, Brenk, Conte,
Gransden, and Tatum study imitation by Vergil of earlier writers, while
most of the contributors to Bernard's volume and the books by Bono,
Kallendorf, Macdonald, Quint, and Rosenberg consider imitation of Vergil
by later writers. Articles by Bulger, Rostvig, Silberman, and Suzuki
examine Spenser's response to his sources, and Quilligan's book looks at
Milton's response to Spenser. Yet with all this critical attention to
imitation, no one except me has proposed that The Faerie Queene's historical passages owe their forms, themes, and narrative functions to the
Aeneid.[5] Even as critics in the past ten years have independently

arrived at many of my interpretations of each poem's historical passages,
my understanding of the poems' relation to each other has remained unique.

Notes

[1] The additional bibliography beginning on page 182 lists all works discussed in this preface and these notes. Criticism that is listed in the additional bibliography but not discussed here illuminates the historical passages or their contexts without directly addressing the issues my dissertation addresses.

[2] For example, Holt declares himself influenced by the Harvard school, with reservations, and Heiden arrives at an extremely negative reading of the Aeneid, by means of an interpretation of the Hercules episode in Book VIII exactly opposite the one I give in Chapter 3.

[3] Some recent critics claim that the visit to the Underworld can have no effect on Aeneas because he does not remember making it; Gotoff feels that the visit is real but that Aeneas must forget it lest he be discouraged by the negative aspects of Rome's future history, whereas Michels interprets the visit as a dream from which Aeneas awakes without any memory of it.

[4] The Vergilian Griffin, for example, mentions that the disappearance of Turnus in Aeneid IX "looks forward to the magical events of the Italian epics of Spenser's Faerie Queene" (95), while the Spenserian Leslie argues that allusions to Aeneid XII in Faerie Queene II.viii are the key to understanding Arthur's combat with Pyrochles and Cymochles (92-98).

[5] Admittedly, Bono assumes that Faerie Queene III.iii imitates Aeneid VI. She refers to Merlin's prophecy as "an appropriately lightened version of Aeneas' underworld vision" (76); in support of her assertion that "Britomart's feminine epic quest differs pervasively in tone from its Vergilian model," she remarks, "One need only contrast the amusingly archaic fairy-tale terrors that surround Merlin with the real horror of Aeneas' descent" (77). Clearly, we agree only on what Spenser's source was, not on what Spenser did with it.

Introduction

When Books I-III of The Faerie Queene were published in 1590, the
volume contained dedicatory and commendatory sonnets, which usually
accompanied new works of literature in Elizabethan England, and a
prefatory letter by Edmund Spenser, addressed to Sir Walter Raleigh
and entitled "A Letter of the Authors expounding his whole intention
in the course of this worke: which for that it giveth great light to
the Reader, for the better understanding is hereunto annexed." In
this letter, Spenser claims that he has "followed all the antique Poets
historicall" and lists Homer, Vergil, Ariosto, and Tasso. He praises
all four of his models primarily for creating morally and politically
exemplary characters:[1]

> [F]irst Homere, who in the Persons of Agamemnon and
> Ulysses hath ensampled a good governour and a vertuous
> man, the one in his Ilias, the other in his Odysseis:
> then Virgil, whose like intention was to doe in the
> person of Aeneas: after him Ariosto comprised them
> both in his Orlando: and lately Tasso dissevered them
> againe, and formed both parts in two persons, namely
> that part which they in Philosophy call Ethice, or
> vertues of a private man, coloured in his Rinaldo:
> The other named Politice in his Godfredo.

The didactic purpose of the heroic poem justifies its departures from
strict historical accuracy, since the poet may need to invent incidents
in order to reveal his hero's virtues or suppress incidents in order to
conceal his vices. Indeed, Spenser calls The Faerie Queene "an historicall fiction" and admits to inventing Arthur's visit to Faeryland and
everything which happens there. Evidently, Spenser considered any

1

fiction featuring a historical character to be a historical poem.

Yet there is another sense in which Vergil, Ariosto, Tasso, and Spenser wrote historical poems. Unlike Homer, each of these poets included partial accounts of his country's history in his poem. The Aeneid contains a prophecy which presents historical figures from Aeneas' time to Vergil's, and a shield which displays events from Romulus' infancy to Augustus' triple triumph. Orlando Furioso, in five historical passages, covers the House of Este from the Carolingian era to Ariosto's time and French interference in Italian affairs from the sixth century to the sixteenth. Gerusalemme Liberata complements Ariosto's work by covering the ancestors of the Estensi from the fall of the Roman Empire to the First Crusade and adding the Estean ruler of Tasso's generation. The Faerie Queene contains a chronicle of British history from the first settlers to the death of Uther Pendragon and a prophecy of rulers and events from Arthur's successor to the reign of Elizabeth Tudor. These historical passages serve a variety of extra-literary purposes. Praise of the poet's patron and ruler occurs in each work; local history undoubtedly interested, entertained, and instructed each poem's original audience; some of the passages seem designed to educate the ruler in the nature of good government; and some promote national pride and patriotic fervor.

This last purpose appears much more clearly in Vergil's and Spenser's poems than in Ariosto's or Tasso's. With one exception, the historical passages in the Italian poems appeal to the urban and familial loyalties which characterized the Renaissance city-state. That exception, Ariosto's description of French invasions of Italy, encourages enmity toward the

French but not solidarity among the Italians. In contrast, Vergil's historical passages show Rome becoming the capital first of a unified Italy and then of an empire including all the known world, in which citizens owe their allegiance and service to the State that the ruler governed and represented, rather than to the person of the ruler himself. Likewise, the chronicle in The Faerie Queene tells the story of the kingdom as a whole, although the prophecy focuses more narrowly on the Britons, dismissing Saxons, Danes, and Normans as usurpers in order to present the accession of Henry VII as the restoration of the legitimate royal line.

The extent to which Vergil and Spenser possessed similar attitudes toward their countries perhaps derives from the similarity of their countries' circumstances. In both cases, prolonged struggles with rival powers first produced a sense of national identity; the Punic Wars unified Italy under Rome's leadership, as the Hundred Years' War united the English barons behind their monarch. Subsequently, traumatic periods of internal strife increased the citizens' consciousness of their essential unity and taught them to value peace. Much of the praise Augustus received came from gratitude for his ending the civil wars promptly and decisively, while Henry VII's resolution of the Wars of the Roses won for the Tudor family a loyalty great enough to survive two generations' religious and political reversals of policy. In Augustan Rome and in Elizabethan England, political stability and economic prosperity combined to create a climate in which literature and the other arts flourished, so that many poets in both periods described their times as a golden age.

In our time, however, able to look back on the end of the Augustan
and Elizabethan eras, we may not feel inclined to share Vergil's and
Spenser's enthusiasm. Furthermore, much of the content of their historical passages, especially in Spenser's case, has become unfamiliar as
historians have discovered its inaccuracy. Some twentieth-century
critics have condemned these passages as irrelevant both to a modern
audience and to the poems themselves. The Aeneid has generally been
less subject to this criticism than The Faerie Queene, whose admirers
have rarely hesitated to deplore what they consider boring and pointless
digressions in an otherwise excellent work. This dissertation not only
defends the historical material in The Faerie Queene against the charge
of irrelevance, but also shows that Spenser borrowed from Vergil the
techniques for making history an integral part of a heroic poem. To
prove these points, the first four chapters consider the four historical
passages in the Aeneid and The Faerie Queene, discussing especially the
narrative context and function of each. A fifth chapter considers whether
Aristo and Tasso use history in analogous ways and concludes that the
Aeneid must have served as Spenser's primary model for the integration
of historical material with the fictions of The Faerie Queene.

Note

1. Edmund Spenser, <u>The Faerie Queene</u>, ed. Thomas P. Roche, Jr.
(New York: Penguin, 1978), p. 15.

Chapter 1

THE EFFECT OF ANCHISES' PROPHECY ON AENEAS

Vergil's readers generally agree that Aeneas changes in the course of the _Aeneid_, however differently they define the nature and extent of that change. Pöschl, for example, denies any psychological development but admits an increase in heroic stature and inner strength, caused by the Romanization of Aeneas' values.[1] Parry argues that Aeneas sacrifices all his heroic and human qualities to a glorious but impersonal destiny, while Lewis claims that he matures into full humanity as he learns to reconcile his passions with his vocation.[2] The critics also disagree as to when Aeneas changes, with arguments for the process continuing throughout the first half of the poem, for its taking place in the four central books (V-VIII), and for its being restricted to Book VI.[3] Despite these areas of dispute, commentators are in complete agreement on one point: that Anchises' prophecy is a crucial part of the process.

In order to assess the effect Anchises' prophecy has, we must decide how Aeneas changes and how much of that change occurs during his visit to Hades. A comparison of his first speech in Book I with his first speech in Book VII suggests the extent to which his attitudes have altered in the first half of the _Aeneid_. His initial speech is a soliloquy, delivered during a severe sea storm, in which he envies those who died "before their fathers' eyes, under Troy's lofty walls" (ante ora patrum Troiae sub moenibus altis, 1.95). He laments that

6

Diomedes did not kill him there,

> where fierce Hector lies, thanks to Achilles' spear,
> where huge Sarpedon lies, where the Simois rolls so
> many men's stolen shields and helmets and strong bodies
> beneath its waves!
>
> saevus ubi Aeacidae telo iacet Hector, ubi ingens
> Sarpedon, ubi tot Simois correpta sub undis
> scuta virum galeasque et fortia corpora volvit!
> (1.99-101)

Apparently Aeneas does not fear death so much as he regrets living. He still grieves for fallen Troy, its heroes slain and its river choked with corpses. In imminent danger of drowning, he mourns for a past he has already lost rather than for the future he is about to forfeit.

In Book VII, Aeneas first speaks to interpret an omen. Their eating the loaves of bread which they had used as plates prompts Ascanius to say that they are eating their tables. Immediately Aeneas interrupts his son, recognizing the predicted sign. After greeting the promised land and the Penates, he announces, "This is our home, this is our fatherland" (hic domus, haec patria est, 7.122). He explains that Anchises had bequeathed him the interpretation of this omen, and he gives his followers instructions:

> Gladly, with the first light of the sun, let us find out
> what places these are, what people live here, and where
> their city is. . . .
>
>   primo laeti cum lumine solis
> quae loca, quive habeant homines, ubi moenia gentis,
> vestigemus. . . .   (7.130-32)

Clearly Aeneas accepts as his new home a country of which he knows nothing save that it was prophesied. He had filled his first speech in Book I with proper names from the Trojan past, but in Book VII he eagerly plans to learn what names belong to his future homeland. Admittedly,

the difference in his circumstances undoubtedly accounts for much of
the alteration in his mood. His opening soliloquy occurred during a
sea storm raised by Aeolus at Juno's request, while this speech occurs
during the calm before the analogous human storm which Allecto raises
for Juno. Yet the altered circumstances cannot fully explain the change
in Aeneas' attitude. He had been committed to fallen Troy but has
become committed to an Italian future. An examination of his behavior
in Books I-V will make it clear how much of that change occurs before
Aeneas visits his father's shade in Hades.

The sea storm in _Aeneid_ I blows the Trojan ships off course,
forcing them to the Libyan coast. There Dido, queen of the recently
founded city of Carthage, offers the Aeneadae food, shelter, and a
permanent home if they wish to settle there. At her request, Aeneas
tells the story of Troy's fall and his subsequent wanderings. Throughout his tale, which occupies Books II and III, Aeneas receives commands
and directions from many supernatural sources: ghosts, gods, oracles,
and visions. Unfortunately, he often disregards the commands and mis-
understands the directions. His mistaken responses are due, at least
in part, to that yearning for the lost past and lack of confidence in
the promised future which we saw in his opening soliloquy.

As the Greeks attacked Troy, the shade of Hector appears to Aeneas,
ordering him to find a new home for the Trojan gods. Hector describes
the crisis vividly: Troy in flames, Priam in danger, the citadel of
Pergamus doomed to destruction (2.289-92). These lines bristle with
proper names, in contrast to the instructions which follow: "seek the
great walls which you will found at last, after wandering across the

sea" (<u>moenia quaere</u> / <u>magna pererrato statues quae denique ponto</u>, 2.294-95). Moved by this news of Troy's immediate peril, Aeneas ignores Hector's orders and hastens into the fray.[4] Although Aeneas prefers to fight to the death, the gods have assigned him the more arduous task of survival, as his vision of Hector indicated. His divine mother, Venus, therefore appears to Aeneas at Priam's palace and tells him to go home. She refrains from prophesying to him, perhaps because he is not yet willing to accept responsibility for the future. Instead, she reminds him of his duty to protect his family (2.594-600) and then reveals the gods who are destroying Troy (2.601-623), a sight which relieves Aeneas of his duty to defend his city. <u>Pietas</u> might call for a man to die opposing Greeks, but it forbids him to oppose the gods.[5]

Once home, Aeneas has difficulty persuading his father, Anchises, to leave their native country, but Jupiter sends omens which convince the old man to accompany his son. As they flee the burning city, Aeneas becomes separated from his wife, Creusa. Forgetful of his own safety and of his divinely ordained task, he plunges back into the ruins to search for her. A huge, shadowy image of her suddenly blocks his way and gives him more detailed information about his future:

> A long exile for you, a vast plain of sea to be plowed--
> then you will find the Hesperian land where Lydian Tiber
> flows in calm procession between fields fruitful with men.
> There happy fortunes and a kingdom for you, and a king's
> daughter to be your wife.

> longa tibi exsilia et vastum maris aequor arandum,
> et terram Hesperiam venies, ubi Lydius arva
> inter opima virum leni fluit agmine Thybris.
> illic res laetae regnumque et regia coniunx
> parta tibi.   (2.780-84)

Furthermore, Creusa explains that she must remain to serve Cybele, the
Great Mother, who will keep her safe from harm. In response to Creusa's
speech, Aeneas repeatedly attempts to embrace her shadowy form (2.790-94);
only after she vanishes does he return to the Trojans who have escaped
capture. Grief for the wife he has just lost overwhelms her promise
that he will gain another wife, just as loyalty to the city under attack
caused him to ignore Hector's words about the settlement he will found.
Yet now he does know three important things: he must sail to his new
home; it lies in the west;[6] and it will be a land worth reaching, where
he will be a king. In showing him the gods' hostility to Troy, Venus
began weaning Aeneas from his old patriotism. Creusa's prophecy begins
winning him to a new one.

The Aeneadae first attempt to settle in Thrace, to the northwest
across the Aegean Sea, but they discover that Thracian soil has been
polluted by the murder of a previous Trojan guest. Shaken by this
experience, Aeneas consults the oracle at Delos. His prayer that Apollo
may preserve "the second citadel of Troy" (altera Troiae / Pergama,
3.86-87) indicates that he thinks of the present and the future as
continuous with the past. In response, the god offers a riddle and a
prophecy:

> Hardy Dardanians, the earth that first bore you from the
> stock of your ancestors, that same earth will welcome you,
> restored, to her glad breast. Seek out your ancient mother.
> Here Aeneas' family, both his sons' sons and those who are
> born from them, will be lords over all lands.
>
> Dardanidae duri, quae vos a stirpe parentum
> prima tulit tellus, eadem vos ubere laeto
> accipiet reduces. antiquam exquirite matrem.

> hic domus Aeneae cunctis dominabitur oris
> et nati natorum et qui nascentur ab illis. (3.94-98)

Apollo promises a different kind of continuity from that envisioned by Aeneas. The oracle alludes to a more distant past than the Trojan one Aeneas treasures and predicts apparently unending and unbounded future dominion for his descendants. Troy will prove to have been merely a brief interruption to the relationship between this nameless land and Aeneas' people. For the moment, however, the riddle engages Aeneas' interest more than the prophecy does. Anchises observes that Teucer, the Trojans' earliest ancestor, came from Crete, as did the fertility goddess Cybele, the Great Mother. Since the oracle described the land both as "first" and as a "mother," Anchises confidently identifies it as Crete (3.102-13).[7]

Anchises has overlooked the obvious clue supplied by the patronymic Dardanidae. When the Cretan colony must be abandoned on account of plague, the Penates, Troy's household gods, appear to Aeneas in a dream to reinterpret the Delian oracle. They point out that Dardanus, another founder of Troy, came from a land known as Hesperia to the Greeks and Italy to the Oenotrians who have settled there, a land also called Ausonia (3.161-71). The Penates also supplement Apollo's prophecy with one of their own:

> We shall bear your future offspring to the stars and
> give their city an empire. Prepare great walls for great
> men and do not abandon your weary task in exile.

> idem venturos tollemus in astra nepotes
> imperiumque urbi dabimus. tu moenia magnis
> magna para longumque fugae ne linque laborem.
> (3.158-60)

The household gods promise three things the Delian prediction had not mentioned: deification for some of Aeneas' descendants, an empire for them to rule, and the Penates' assistance in obtaining these things. Moreover, the household gods apparently consider their long-range prophecy to be capable of compensating for the tiresome years of wandering, capable of inspiring Aeneas to continue.

On their way to Italy, the Aeneadae stop at Buthrotum to visit a Trojan settlement ruled by Helenus and Andromache. Helenus, a priest and seer, delivers the most practical prophecy Aeneas receives on his journey, offering specific instructions for minimizing both natural and supernatural dangers. Most helpfully, he predicts an omen, a white sow with thirty suckling piglets, which will mark the site of their city in Italy (3.381-87), warnings against the Greek colonies on the Italian peninsula (3.396-402), and advice as to the safest sea route (3.410-32). In the realm of the supernatural, Helenus explains the correct method of sacrificing (3.403-09), the necessity of propitiating Juno (3.433-40), and the desirability of consulting the Cumaean Sybil (3.441-60). Thanks to this detailed and pragmatic prophecy, Aeneas now knows exactly how to reach his destined home. However, he still believes that his destiny is to recreate Troy in Italy, as Helenus and Andromache have at Buthrotum. They rule over a miniature copy of the fallen city, complete with a citadel called Pergamus, a stream named Xanthus, and Scaean gates (3.349-51). Aeneas envies them their nostalgic replicas and looks forward to replicating Troy on Tiber's banks (3.493-505). He does not yet realize that he must found a new city instead of rebuilding the old one.

The Aeneadae follow Helenus' directions as far as Sicily, but on their way across the Tyrrhenian sea they encounter the great storm which Juno persuaded Aeolus to stir up. As we have seen, Aeneas' thoughts during this crisis are all of fallen Troy, where he wishes he had died. What he has learned of the future has not yet inspired him sufficiently to compensate for what he has lost in the past. Nevertheless, we must not judge him harshly on that account. The gods have deprived Aeneas of his king, his country, and his wife; they have given him commands which he could not interpret correctly; they have permitted Anchises to die in Sicily, although Aeneas was accustomed to rely on his father's guidance; and finally, just when he approached his destination, they have let this storm threaten his survival, scatter his ships, and blow him off the course they had set for him. To hearten him through these trials, they have predicted that he will find a new country, acquire a new wife, and become a king. Only the Penates' prophecy has suggested that the future will be superior to or even different from the past, and their brief mention of apotheoses and an empire for Aeneas' descendants did not take hold of his imagination. To the best of his knowledge, his efforts will result at most in an inferior copy of his former city, a miniature Troy like the one at Buthrotum. Aeneas does not yet understand why the gods seem so determined for him to accomplish this difficult and unrewarding task, but then they have not yet shown him the glorious consequences of his perseverance.

Under the circumstances, Aeneas lands in Libya in an emotionally vulnerable state, certainly tired and worried, probably somewhat resentful. Venus, disguised as a huntress, appears to direct him to

the city of Carthage and to tell him about its queen, Dido. Aeneas
recognizes his mother only as she turns away from him, but she vanishes
before he can embrace her. He reproaches her bitterly for her behavior
(1.407-09), which seems like insult added to injury. In this mood, he
comes to the newly founded city, still under construction. Here he
sees the work he has yet to start proceeding smoothly, and the prospect
immediately appeals to him, as his exclamation reveals: "O fortunate
people, whose walls already rise!" (o fortunati, quorum iam moenia
surgunt! 1.437). When he finds the temple of Juno decorated with
scenes from the Trojan War, he views the pictures as evidence that the
Carthaginians pity Troy's sufferings (1.459-63).[8] Finally, still
wrapped in a cloud of invisibility supplied by Venus, he watches Dido
receiving the captains of ships he had feared lost and hears her offering to share her city with his followers. Before he even speaks with
her himself, then, Aeneas feels immensely grateful to Dido for her
compassion and generosity, qualities he has not recently encountered.
Moreover, he recognizes her as her counterpart; also an exile from
a much-loved homeland, Dido has lost her husband, led her people to
a new country, and founded a city over which she now rules. Aeneas
feels admiration as well as gratitude toward the queen and easily
sympathizes with her. The goddesses who promote his love affair have
ulterior motives--Venus wishes to ensure the Carthaginians' good treatment of her son, while Juno hopes to keep Aeneas in Carthage permanently
so that its destined destruction by Rome will not take place--but
Aeneas' affection for Dido does not result from calculation of any
sort. Here he has everything the gods had promised him: a city to

build, a woman to love, and a kingship in fact, if not in title.
Understandably, he sees no reason to seek out unknown versions of the
things he presently enjoys.

Jupiter sees the situation quite differently, however, and dis-
patches Mercury to rebuke Aeneas. The messenger god argues that Aeneas
owes the prophesied future to his son:

> Consider Ascanius growing up, consider your hopes for
> Iulus, your heir, to whom the kingdom of Italy and the
> Roman land are due.

> Ascanium surgentem et spes heredis Iuli
> respice, cui regnum Italiae Romanaque tellus
> debetur.   4.274-76)

Jupiter's intervention reveals to Aeneas the extent to which he is
committed, whatever he prefers, to the future predicted to him. Apparently, he has no choice about where to settle, and the gods allow him
little leeway as to when to get there. At this crucial moment, Mercury
uses the phrase Romana tellus. This expression is the first indication
Aeneas receives that the Trojan settlement in Italy will not bear the
name of Troy. Aeneas' last conversation with Dido includes a comparison
of his loyalty to the past with his commitment to the future, in which
he does not once refer to the Italian venture in terms of recreating
Ilium. Had he been free to choose his own course of action, he explains,
he would have remained at the site of Troy, restoring Priam's lofty
roofs and the citadel of Pergamus (4.342-44). "But now great Italy,"
he continues, is his fate, and through the remainder of his speech the
new land's names echo: Ausonia, Hesperia, and, repeatedly, Italia
(4.345-61). Never again does he speak of a second Troy for himself.
Although Aeneas still has not had a clear vision of the city he will

found, Mercury's appearance has made him aware of its differences from Troy and its importance to Olympus. Henceforth he begins relinquishing the past and turns with increasing confidence toward the future.

The Aeneadae stop in Sicily to celebrate funeral games on the anniversary of Anchises' death. During the games, Juno's servant Iris maddens the Trojan women into burning the ships. Although Jupiter sends rain to extinguish the flames, Aeneas loses four ships. He also realizes how weary of traveling many of his followers have become. Despite his newly acquired sense of his mission's importance, Aeneas considers staying in Sicily instead of continuing on to Italy (5.700-03). One of the Trojan elders, Nautes, advises him to leave those who prefer settling in Sicily and to take with him only those who volunteer to go on. He suggests that Aeneas could lay out a town for the settlers, naming it Acesta in honor of the Sicilian king, Acestes (5.704-18). Still uncertain, Aeneas sleeps on the decision and has a vision of his father's shade. Anchises tells him to follow Nautes' advice (5.728-31) and to come to the Elysian Fields with the Cumaean Sibyl (5.731-36), where Anchises will prophesy to him: "you will learn of all your posterity and the walls which are granted to you" (genus omne tuum et quae dentur moenia disces, 5.737). Aeneas wakes with restored confidence, consults Acestes, and marks the boundaries of the settlement, calling its districts Troy and Ilium (5.756). Thus he leaves behind a nostalgic replica of the kind he had admired at Buthrotum and hoped to found himself. His action indicates his awareness that the gods do not intend for him to recreate the past. Now he must learn from Anchises in the Underworld about the future they have planned for him and his descendants.

Looking back, we can see that the despair Aeneas voiced in his opening soliloquy had several causes. Emotionally, Aeneas longed for fallen Troy, which he knew to be irrecoverable, and for its promised replacement, which he feared would prove unattainable. Intellectually, he did not yet comprehend the nature of his task or its importance to the gods. Mercury's appearance at Carthage convinced Aeneas that his mission mattered to the Olympians, assured him that he would complete it successfully, and implied that the result would not merely replicate what he had lost. His vision of Anchises gave him further assurance of success and encouraged him to leave behind those who preferred the past to the future. During his visit to the Underworld, Aeneas will finally and completely let go of Troy and all his attempts to recreate it and will discover the eventual consequences of his mission. In Book III of The Faerie Queene, Britomart despairs of life for many of the same reasons as did Aeneas. She suffers from a longing which she believes doomed to frustration, and she understands neither the nature of her love nor its place in the divine plan. Her nurse assures her that her love is acceptable and convinces her that her beloved is attainable. Merlin then teaches her the role her love plays in God's design for British history and predicts the long-range consequences of her marriage. The major difference between Aeneas and Britomart is that Spenser's heroine has no former love to renounce; she needs only to realize that this first love constitutes her duty. Vergil's hero, however, has had two tasks: to stop loving the objects of his past allegiance and to find the destined objects of his future loyalty and love. Aeneas will largely complete both tasks in _Aeneid_ VI.

At the beginning of Book VI, Aeneas reaches Cumae. There he
prays that "Trojan fortune may have followed us only this far" (_hac
Troiana tenus fuerit fortuna secuta_, 6.62). He both hopes that the
ill-luck and enmity which have pursued the Trojans will cease and
indicates his willingness to let go of Troy entirely. However, the
Sibyl prophesies a repetition of the Trojan War, with another Xanthus
and Simois, a Doric camp, a Latin Achilles, and the cause of conflict
again a foreign bride (6.86-94). Evidently Aeneas, forbidden to rebuild
his former city, must still relive its battles. Yet he remains unmoved
by the Sibylline oracle, since he has anticipated this combat (6.103-05),
which Anchises' shade had hinted might occur (5.730-31). Aeneas proceeds to ask the Sibyl to take him through Hades to visit Anchises
(6.106-23). In making this request and throughout his conversation
with the Sibyl, Aeneas sounds primarily interested in the future, in
the Italian war and in Anchises' promised prophecy. Nevertheless, his
first three encounters with shades in the Underworld will force him
to recall and permanently relinquish everything he has loved and lost
in the past.

As he and the Sibyl approach the river Styx, Aeneas recognizes
the shade of his helmsman, Palinurus, who had fallen overboard on the
voyage from Sicily to Italy. Palinurus asks Aeneas either to find and
bury his body, which lies on an Italian beach, or to arrange for his
shade to cross the river despite his body's remaining unburied (6.365-
71). He calls Aeneas "unvanquished" (_invicte_, 6.365) and prays that

the hero will help him for Anchises' sake and "for the hope of Iulus, growing up" (per spes surgentis Iuli, 6.364). By so praying, Palinurus not only echoes Mercury's speech to Aeneas at Carthage (Ascanium surgentem et spes heredis Iuli, 4.274), but also assumes that an appeal to the hero's hopes for the future will prove more effective than one based on their relationship in the past. Although the Sibyl rebukes the helmsman for his presumption, she does console him by predicting that the coast where he died will forever bear his name (6.372-81). Palinurus "rejoices in that name for the land" (gaudet cognomine terra, 6.383), and the Sibyl leads Aeneas down to the river's edge to board the ferryboat.[9]

Aeneas next sees Dido's shade, in the Mourning Fields where those who died for love wander eternally. Weeping while he speaks, he laments her death, explains again how reluctantly he left her at the gods' bidding, and begs her to speak to him (6.455-68). Dido silently turns away to join her husband, Sychaeus, who returns her love (6.469-74).[10]

> Nonetheless, shocked by her unfair fate, Aeneas follows
> her for a long time with tears and grieves at her going.
>
> nec minus Aeneas casu percussus iniquo
> prosequitur lacrimis longe et miseratur euntem.
> (6.475-76)

Painful as Aeneas found it to leave Dido in Carthage, he finds their final parting even harder to bear. Then he could hope she might live happily without him; now he must accept the fact that she chose to die instead. He had left her on account of his duty, which included a new marriage; now she rejects him in favor of her old marriage and duty she owes Sychaeus. Yet Dido's rejection of him, although Aeneas does not appreciate it, sets him free to continue on the course the gods have decreed for him, as Vergil's next line suggests: "Thereafter, he exerted himself on his assigned path" (Inde datum molitur iter, 6.477). Aeneas' "assigned path" refers to his destiny as well as to the road which he must follow through the Underworld. It takes some effort for him to go on after leaving Dido for the last time, but she left him freer to make that effort than before.

The last shade Aeneas meets before he arrives in the Elysian Fields is that of Deiphobus, the Trojan prince who married Helen after the death of Paris. He tells Aeneas how he died on the night Troy fell (6.509-30) and asks what has brought his former comrade to Hades (6.531-34). But time passes quickly while they talk, as the Sibyl reminds Aeneas (6.535-43). Deiphobus assures her that he will return to his accustomed place among the shades of famous warriors. He then bids Aeneas goodbye: "Go, our glory, go; make use of better fates" (i decus, i, nostrum; melioribus utere fatis, 6.546). This farewell both associates Aeneas with the Trojans by calling him "our glory" and distinguishes him from Deiphobus and Troy by assuming his fate will prove better than theirs.

These three encounters recapitulate Aeneas' history from the fall of Troy to his landing in Italy, although not chronologically. Aeneas meets the shades in the reverse order from that in which they had died, for Palinurus fell overboard near the end of Book V, Dido's suicide closed Book IV, and Menelaus slew Deiphobus during Troy's final battle, which Aeneas narrated in Book II. Each figure stands for a period in the hero's life: Deiphobus for the Trojan War, Palinurus for all the subsequent voyages, and Dido for the time spent in Carthage.[11] More

specifically, each represents a threat to the successful completion of
Aeneas' task. Deiphobus' death recalls Aeneas' desire to die fighting
for Troy; the helmsman's loss reminds us that Aeneas often tried to
settle in the wrong place because he lacked sufficient guidance to
reach the right one and because he wearied of traveling; and his own
affection for Dido and her city delayed his proceeding to his destined
bride and kingdom. Most importantly, however, each encounter directs
Aeneas away from the past which that shade symbolizes and toward the
future to which he belongs. Palinurus appeals to him in the name of
his hopes for that future; Dido's rejection of his love furthers the
process of freeing him which his leaving her had begun; and Deiphobus
explicitly sends him forward to make use of better fortunes than he
had known in the past.[12] It remains only for Anchises to reveal the
form of that future to Aeneas.

Aeneas finds his father surveying a great crowd of heroic shades.
Anchises explains that they await their turn to drink from the river
of forgetfulness and receive new bodies (6.713-15). Indeed, these
souls will become Aeneas' descendants in Italy (6.716-18). Aeneas
asks for and receives a fuller explanation of reincarnation (6.719-
51); then Anchises leads him and the Sibyl into the crowd and onto a
mound whence they can review the figures which pass by (6.752-55).

Anchises' survey has two main sections, with an epilogue in praise
of the Marcelli.[13] In the first part he points out certain Alban
kings, Romulus, and Augustus (6.756-807). Place names abound, for
this passage concentrates on the establishment of townships and the
conquest of lands. Roman kings and Republicans occupy the second part

of Anchises' speech, and this section emphasizes the character rather than the geographical extent of the Roman achievement (6.808-853). Anchises refers to the Trojan past rarely in his revelation of the Italian future, and those few allusions almost all concern genealogy.[14]

Although three hundred and thirty years separate Aeneas' death from Romulus' founding the city of Rome (1.267-77),[15] Anchises names only five rulers of Alba Longa. Of these, Aeneas' son Silvius (6.760-66) and grandson Silvius Aeneas (6.768-70) receive the fullest descriptions; Anchises barely names the others. He groups all five then with a crowd of youths crowned with oak leaves, the founders of the towns of Nomentum, Gabii, Fidena, Collatia, Pometii, Castrum Inui, Bola, and Cora. Anchises thus identifies half again as many settlements as he does kings. The ringing roll-call ends with a reminder: "Then these will be names; now they are lands without a name" (haec tum nomina erunt, nunc sunt sine nomine terrae, 6.776). The prophecies in Books II and III named Aeneas' destination, sometimes ambiguously or obscurely, but at last by multiple names. Anchises' final sentence here could serve as a summary of that earlier process. Aeneas' goal originally had no name and he needed to find names for it so that he might settle there; his descendants need to settle and thereby name the sites in that land which have no names as yet. Names confer reality on things; the process Anchises describes makes Italy more real to Aeneas and reinforces the distinction between the Trojan and Hellenic past and the Italic future.

The subordination of persons to places continues with the treatment of Romulus and Rome. Romulus receives four lines, mostly concerned with his parentage (6.777-80). Rome merits seven lines, including an epic simile (6.781-87). Since Aeneas has not yet heard about the great city, Anchises compares it to something Aeneas already understands:

> And Rome will encircle her seven summits with one wall,
> blest in her race of men: just as the Berecynthian mother,
> turret-crowned, is carried on her chariot through Phrygian
> cities, joyous in her progeny of gods, a hundred offspring
> in her embrace, all heaven-dwellers, all occupying the lofty
> heavens above.

> septemque una sibi muro circumdabit arces,
> felix prole virum: qualis Berecyntia mater
> invehitur curru Phrygias turrita per urbes
> laeta deum partu, centum complexa nepotes,
> omnis caelicolas, omnis supera alta tenentes.
>   (6.783-87)

The Trojans had worshipped the Great Mother in Asia Minor, as the phrase "Phrygian cities" reminds us. She kept Creusa in Troy to serve her (2.788) and she will prevent Turnus from burning the ships made from her sacred trees (9.77-125). Aeneas continues to pray to her during crises after he arrives in Italy (7.139, 10.252-55). Her familiarity and Aeneas' high regard for her make the comparison most appropriate.

Having described the city of Rome, Anchises says, "Observe this race, your Romans" (hanc aspice gentem / Romanosque tuos, 6.788-89). Temporarily ignoring more than seven hundred years of Roman history, he immediately singles out Augustus Caesar.[16] Augustus will fulfill the predictions Aeneas has received previously: "This man, this is the one whom you have so often heard promised to you" (hic vir, hic est, tibi quem promitti saepius audis, 6.791). Specifically, he fulfills the Delian oracle's prophecy that Aeneas' family will rule over all the earth's boundaries (3.97). According to Anchises, the Augustan

empire includes the Africans and Indians and extends beyond the zone
of the Zodiac, beyond the route followed by the sun, where Atlas
stands holding up the heavens (6.794-97). Augustus' approach frightens
the distant lands around the Caspian Sea and Lake Maeotis and troubles
the mighty waters of the Nile (6.798-800). From Alba Longa Aeneas'
progeny will settle Italy, but from Rome his greatest descendant
will govern the world. The process of geographical expansion can go
no further.

Anchises completes his description of the empire's extent by
turning from geography to mythology. He claims that the Greek Hercules
and Bacchus did not traverse as much of the earth as Roman Augustus
will rule (6.801-05). This comparison, like the Cybele simile, sets
a Roman equal to the gods. Moreover, Hercules was a man who became
a god, as Anchises says Romulus will (6.780). Both Hercules and
Romulus become gods for two reasons, their merit and their divine parentage. Augustus is likewise a god's son (divi genus, 6.792), he expands
Romulus' city into a universal empire, and he surpasses Hercules in
the extent of his beneficent influence. Anchises predicts that he
will restore to Latium the golden age it enjoyed under Saturn--i.e.,
he will govern as only a god had before him. The implication that
apotheosis awaits Augustus is inescapable. Thus he, with Romulus, will
fulfill the Penates' prophecy that Aeneas' descendants shall become
divine (3.158).

Anchises concludes the first section of his speech with a question
for Aeneas:

> Do we still doubt we should extend our power by deeds,
> or does fear forbid us to settle on Ausonian land?
>
> et dubitamus adhuc virtutem extendere factis,
> aut metus Ausonia prohibet consistere terra? (6.806-07)

Anchises intends this part of the Review of Heroes to encourage Aeneas
during the coming war in two ways. The deeds of his descendants depend
on his completing his own task successfully, and so Anchises' description of their action implies that Aeneas will succeed. His offspring
also set Aeneas a good example. They plant towns throughout Latium
and found a city as great as Rome, as if to show him how easily he may
settle in his new land. Their acts establish a world-wide empire and
in some cases win them divine honors, thus suggesting that exercising
one's abilities receives due reward. Anchises evidently assumes that
his discourse has the desired effect, as he continues without giving
Aeneas an opportunity to answer his rhetorical question.

The second section of Anchises' revelation begins with the figure
of Numa Pompilius, Rome's second king. Anchises describes him as a
Roman priest ready to offer sacrifice,[17] as the first law-giver, and
as a man who will rise from poverty to great dominion (6.808-12). Next
comes Tullus Hostilius, who will rouse the men of Rome to military
action (6.12-15). They represent two Roman concepts of duty, one
honoring the gods and laws, the other serving his homeland in war.
These forms of pietas cannot be separated for Aeneas in the future.
In order to obey the divine commands to settle in Latium, he will need
to resort to arms. The fourth king of Rome offers a negative rather
than a positive example: boastful Ancus, who craves popularity even
among the shades (6.815-16). Anchises has nothing to say about the

Tarquinii and so reaches Brutus, the founder of the Republic (6.817-18).

Although Anchises begins his lecture on great Romans with this detailed and chronological account of Rome's early kings, he surveys the Republic's leaders neither in detail nor chronologically.[18] Instead he alternates between describing one man or one event rather fully and listing individuals and families with little or no information about them. His technique exactly suits the situation: anyone attempting to identify a host of men would pause only occasionally to tell a story about one of them. Anchises' lists presumably do not seem bare to Aeneas, since they are illustrated by the figures he sees. Nevertheless, surely the most affecting moments for him occur when Anchises comments at greater length about some character.

Brutus, the Republic's founder and first consul, has a somewhat disturbing history. "For the sake of lovely liberty" (pulchra pro libertate, 6.821), he will sentence his sons to death for conspiring with the enemy and attempting to restore the monarchy by force of arms (6.819-21). Anchises follows the tale with this comment:

> Tragic man, however posterity shall relate these facts:
> his love of country and great desire for honor shall prevail.
>
> infelix, utcumque ferent ea facta minores:
> vincet amor patriae laudumque immensa cupido.
> (6.822-23)

In Brutus' case, love of country and love for one's offspring will come in conflict. Anchises, in the process of inspiring Aeneas with these two affections, has mixed feelings about Brutus' solution of a conflict between them. He calls the consul infelix because his action will be right for Rome but painful for himself. Moreover, Anchises

ascribes his deed to <u>laudum immensa cupido</u> as well as to <u>amor patriae</u>.
The longing to do praiseworthy deeds is an excellent thing, but eagerness to be praised inspires evil as well as virtuous deeds. The
ambiguity of Anchises' expression reflects the complexity of his
reaction.[19]

By far the longest of Anchises' commentaries concerns Caesar and
Pompey. Although friends in the Underworld, they will wage mighty
war against each other in their future lives (6.826-31). For the first
time Anchises addresses the shades instead of Aeneas:

> Do not, my sons, do not let your souls become accustomed
> to such wars, nor turn your hardy strength against your
> country's entrails; and you first, you who derive from the
> Olympian race, be merciful, throw down the weapons from
> your hand, my kinsman! --
>
> ne, pueri, ne tanta animis adsuescite bella
> neu patriae validas in viscera vertite viris;
> tuque prior, tu parce, genus qui ducis Olympo,
> proice tela manu, sanguis meus! --
>
> (6.832-35)

Here no conflict of interest between familial and patriotic duties
exists. Anchises realizes that civil warfare does nothing but harm to
the contested land, and he alludes to the personal relationship between
Caesar and Pompey which ought to prohibit them from fighting, referring
to them as "the father-in-law" and "the son-in-law" rather than by their
names (<u>socer</u>, 6.830; <u>gener</u>, 6.831). In Brutus' case, Anchises explained
both the cause of the death sentence (<u>nova bella moventis</u>, 6.820) and the
consul's justification for it, but no extenuating phrase such as <u>pulchra</u>
<u>pro libertate</u> appears here. Anchises advances no explanation of the
mutual enmity, takes neither side, and offers no information as to the
outcome of the war. He only pleads with both shades, especially with

that one who will be his lineal descendant. He had pointed them out
initially as "well-matched in arms" (paribus . . . in armis, 6.826),
and his last line suggests that they have already armed themselves for
combat. Then the line breaks off as if in despair. Revealing
descendants to Aeneas may inspire him to act as he has been destined
to, but citing even divine ancestors to Caesar cannot prevent him from
acting as he is destined to. Anchises' entire revelation has family
and country for its two themes, but Brutus' tale indicates that some
men must sacrifice family members for Rome's sake, and the civil war
shows both a family and the country divided against itself. In the
first case, we see the tragedy of an individual: in the second, the
tragedy of a nation.[20]

Anchises passes at once to a contrasting pair of generals. They
will fight in foreign rather than in civil wars, and his tone of pride
in their victories, coming immediately after his plea for an end to
civil strife, makes it clear that Anchises does not condemn all warfare.
He predicts Mummius' capture of Corinth and his Capitoline triumph
first (6.836-37), then turns to Aemilius Paullus:

> That man will destroy Argos and Agamemnon's Mycenae,
> and will slay Aeacides himself, descendant of warlike
> Achilles; he will have avenged his Trojan ancestors and
> Minerva's violated temple.
>
> eruet ille Argos Agamemnoniasque Mycenas
> ipsumque Aeaciden, genus armipotentis Achilli,
> ultus avos Troiae templa et temerata Minervae.
> (6.838-40)

Aemilius Paullus will actually defeat Perseus of Macedon, a very distant
descendant of Achilles, and thereby gain the name "Macedonicus." This
description of that event serves two purposes more important than strict

historical accuracy, however. Like the Cybele simile for Rome, this passage presents something strange to Aeneas in familiar terms. Aeneas can best understand the Roman conquest of the Greek city-states if Anchises explains it as vengeance for the destruction of Troy. Moreover, Anchises' direct address to Caesar and Pompey blurred the chronological relationship between them, throwing the reader momentarily into the first century, but the Homeric terms used in this passage restore us, as well as Aeneas, to the time in which the poem is set.

Near the end of this section, Anchises points to the Scipiones, Scipio Africanus Maior and his grandson, Scipio Africanus Numantinus, whom he calls "two lightning bolts of war" and "Libya's ruin" (duo fulmina belli, 6.842; cladem Libyae, 6.843). Shortly thereafter he turns to Marcellus, who "will subdue the Carthaginians and rebellious Gaul" (sternet Poenos Gallumque rebellem, 6.858). Dido used the names Libya and Poeni for her country and her people in the first speech Aeneas heard her make (1.567-77); he can hardly have forgotten her land and race so soon after seeing her shade in the Fields of Mourning. By including Africa in the Augustan empire, Anchises implied that Rome would conquer Carthage, but these references make explicit to Aeneas the future enmity between his Romans and Dido's Carthaginians. The difference between Aeneas' reaction to meeting Dido's shade and his presumed response to Anchises' prophecy of the Punic Wars indicates the psychological and emotional distance Anchises expects him to have traveled.

Yet the prophecy does not demand that Aeneas turn from past affections to future loyalties without assuring him that the Roman achievement will be worth the price he and others must pay to establish it. Set between the list in which the Scipiones appear and the passage in praise of Marcellus is Anchises' characterization of that achievement. "Others," he says, meaning the Greeks, will remain superior in bronze-casting, marble sculpture, oratory, and astronomy (6.847-50). However, Greek culture will survive and spread only under Roman government, for the Romans will excel in legal and military affairs:

> Remember, Roman, you are to govern the nations in your power
> (these arts will be yours), and impose the habit of peace;
> you are to spare the conquered and wear down the proud with war.

> tu regere imperio populos, Romane, memento
> (hae tibi erunt artes), pacisque imponere morem,
> parcere subiectis et debellare superbos.
>
> (6.851-53)

Romane is perhaps the most surprising word in this sentence. This revelation has an audience within the poem, Aeneas, to whom Anchises speaks, as well as an audience outside the poem, the Romans for whom Vergil writes. Here they merge momentarily. Anchises began the Review of Heroes by identifying "Dardanian progeny" with "the offspring from the Italian race" (Dardaniam prolem . . . Itala de gente nepotes, 6.756-57), and proceeded to introduce the Romans as Aeneas' own people (6.788-89). Now, almost at the end of his speech, he addresses Aeneas as a Roman, as if the process of transferring Aeneas' loyalty to a future city were complete.

Although some critics have found Vergil's description of Rome's "arts" debatable,[21] the function of Anchises' words within the poem is clear. These three lines serve as a final set of directions for Aeneas. Earlier prophecies told him how to reach Italy: this one tells

him what sort of actions he should take there. Simultaneously, the
passage motivates Aeneas by describing the kind of civilication his
actions will help to found. According to Anchises, Rome will have a
peaceful and settled way of life, full of mercy for those who have
been brought low and using might only to humble those who bear themselves too haughtily. Just warfare when necessary, just peace when
possible, and firm government at all times are inspiring goals toward
which to strive, even if they will be achieved only in part and by one's
distant descedants.

In the second section of Anchises' prophecy, Vergil has concentrated
on military figures. Although Rome produced enough victorious generals
for him to paint an exclusively optimistic picture, the poet devoted
more than a third of this section to two tragic stories, those of Brutus
and of Caesar and Pompey. Thus Aeneas can count the cost as well as to
admire the achievements of Roman history. On the one hand, Anchises
makes it clear that Rome will enjoy unprecedented military triumphs;
on the other hand, some Romans will sacrifice personal relationships
either to patriotic duty or to political ambition. Yet, as the description of Rome's arts indicated, Rome's greatness will be not its military
conquests but the civilization it will establish throughout its empire.
Immediately after this inspiring message, Vergil describes Aeneas and
the Sibyl as "those marvelling ones" (haec mirantibus, 6.854), a phrase
which suggests admiration as well as amazement.

After a brief pause, Anchises points out another conquering hero,
Marcus Claudius Marcellus (6.855-59). Aeneas questions him about the
shade he sees accompanying Marcellus (6.860-66), inquiring whether the

young man is the elder's "son, or some other descendant from the great
stock" of that family (_filius, anne aliquis magna de stirpe nepotum_?
6,864). Aeneas' curiosity about the shade's identity and kinship
reveals the extent of his involvement with the historical and genealogical pageant in progress. Anchises explains that Rome will suffer its
greatest sorrow in this youth's untimely death (6.867-74). This shade
will become a man as remarkable for _pietas_ and faith as for strength
and military skill (6.875-81). Only when Anchises addresses the shade
directly does he finally identify the youth as another Marcellus and
beg that he may scatter flowers like a mourner at the young man's
funeral (6.881-86).[22] This speech, which concludes the Review of
Heroes, combines pride in Roman virtues with sorrow for Roman suffering
and thus recalls the second half of Anchises' prophecy.

The two sections of the Review of Heroes complement each other in
many ways. The first half, with its Italian place-names, Romulus'
founding of Rome, Augustus' establishment of an empire, and both rulers'
apotheoses, recalls the prophecies given to Aeneas in Books I-V and
shows how they will be fulfilled. The figures in this section also furnish
Aeneas with examples of successful geographical relocation and settlement, tasks which he has almost despaired of completing. The question
with which Anchises concludes the first half of his prophecy indicates
that he intended it to dispel Aeneas' doubts and fears:

> Do we still doubt we should extend our power by deeds,
> or does fear forbid us to settle on Ausonian land?
>
> et dubitamus adhuc virtutem extendere factis,
> aut metus Ausonia prohibet consistere terra?   (6.806-07)

The second half, with its emphasis on military affairs and its condemnation of civil strife, anticipates the conflict in Latium in Books
VII-XII. This section opens with priestly Numa and valorous Tullus
Hostilius and closes with young Marcellus, who exhibits both reverence
and strength. Although Aeneas has demonstrated his own _pietas_ and
fighting ability earlier in the _Aeneid_, he will function as his
people's priest and general only after their landing at the mouth of
the Tiber in Book VII, and these figures exemplify his future roles.
Just as the first half of the prophecy emphasized the deeds of Aeneas'
descendants and encouraged him to undertake similar deeds, so the second
half emphasized the Romans' virtues and directed him to show similar
virtues. Again, Anchises' concluding lines, which here describe the
arts of Rome, make the message and its intended effect upon Aeneas
clear. Finally, the pairing of the two Marcelli illustrates the dual
nature of warfare, which produces both the victor's joy and the mourner's
sorrow. Aeneas will experience both emotions in the second half of the
poem. Indeed, Anchises' eulogy for young Marcellus, filled with delight
in his descendant's glory and grief at his loss, could serve for any
of those who die young in Books IX-XII: Euryalus, Pallas, Lausus,
Camilla, and especially Turnus.

Throughout the Review of Heroes, Vergil departs from chronological
order and completeness to select only the figures he wants and to put
them in the order he prefers. The necessity of Aeneas' comprehending
the prophecy provides one of the principles of selection; Romans who
will conquer Menelaus' Greece and Dido's Libya receive more attention
than those who will fight in lands unfamiliar to Aeneas. In the first

half of the Review, Vergil omits many of the Alban rulers and all of

the Romans between Romulus and Augustus in order to concentrate on

the founding of towns, of Rome, and of the empire, and in order to

present a wholly positive and inspiring picture. In the prophecy's

second half, Vergil departs from chronological order for a somewhat

different purpose. He moves from the tragic story of patriotic Brutus

to a crowd of happy and patriotic Republicans, reaches the tragic story

of Caesar and Pompey, whose actions hurt rather than help their country,

and concludes with another crowd of happy Republicans, who serve Rome

rather than themselves. These juxtapositions suggest that deeds should

be judged not on the basis of the doers' personal happiness but on the

basis of the deeds' usefulness to Rome, a lesson Aeneas needs to learn

in order to value his past and future losses less than the civilization

he will help establish, the civilization Anchises describes so inspir-

ingly at the end of the Review. Finally, Vergil juxtaposes Marcelli

from the third and first centuries to sum up the prophecy's dual emphasis

on the achievements of Rome and on their cost in human sorrow.

Although Vergil reminds the reader and Anchises informs Aeneas of

the price which has been paid for Rome's greatness, the primary effect

of the prophecy on Aeneas is apparently positive:

> After Anchises led his son through each of these fields,
> and kindled his soul with love of the glory to come,
> then he relates to him the wars to be waged thereafter,
> and tells him of the Laurentian tribes and Latinus' city,
> and which struggle to avoid, which to endure, and how.
>
> quae postquam Anchises natum per singula duxit
> incenditque animum famae venientis amore,
> exim bella viro memorat quae deinde gerenda,

> Laurentisque docet populos urbemque Latini,
> et quo quemque modo fugiatque feratque laborem.
> (6.888-92)

As Aeneas had told Dido and as his own actions indicated, he proceeded
toward Italy not by choice but in obedience to divine commands. The
closer he came geographically, the further his prophesied reward
receded temporally, moving from his own settlement to his descendants'
empire. Anchises brings this distant future into the present for
Aeneas. In a sense, the Review of Heroes does not merely show Aeneas
how the gods' promises will be fulfilled, but actually fulfills them
for him. This vision of Roman history functions as simultaneously
the most remote and the most immediate compensation ever offered to
Aeneas for his obedience. His encounters with Palinurus, Dido, and
Deiphobus had forced him to recall and relinquish his painful memories
of the past, but Anchises' prophecy enables him to comprehend the goal
for which he had left Troy, wandered for years, and abandoned Dido.
Most importantly, the Review of Heroes causes him to feel ardor for
that goal and for its future. As a result of Anchises' revelation,
Aeneas' attitude changes from the grim determination he had shown the
Sibyl at the beginning of Book VI to the ardent interest in Latium
revealed in his first speech in Book VII. Only such a complete commitment, emotional as well as intellectual, would be capable of supporting
Aeneas through the Latin conflict. Grieved both by the pain he inflicts
and by the losses he suffers, he nevertheless endures, to lay the
foundation in Latium for the future greatness of Rome.

Merlin's prophecy, in Book III of The Faerie Queene, resembles
Anchises' revelation in many respects. It, too, divides into two

sections which complement one another. Both Vergil and Spenser select only those figures and events which will best serve their purposes. Vergil abandons chronological order, but remains historically accurate; Spenser presents British history chronologically, but alters the traditional accounts in several places. In both cases, the results have the desired effect upon the listening character. Just as Aeneas leaves the Underworld to accomplish his destined task, Britomart leaves Merlin's cave to accomplish hers. He has had a longer journey, psychologically as well as physically, to complete before he reached the Elysian Fields than she had before she came to Merlin, but the historical prophecies they hear have the same role to play in changing their attitudes and actions.

Notes

1 Viktor Pöschl, _The Art of Vergil_, trans. Gerda Seligson (Ann Arbor: Univ. of Michigan Press, 1962, rpt. 1970), pp. 58-59.

2 Adam Parry, "The Two Voices of Virgil's Aeneid," in _Virgil_, ed. Steele Commager (Englewood Cliffs, N.J.: Prentice-Hall, 1966), p. 118; C. S. Lewis, "Virgil and the Subject of Secondary Epic," in _Virgil_, ed. Commager, pp. 65-66.

3 For example, C. M. Bowra, _From Virgil to Milton_ (London: Macmillan, 1961), p. 63, states that Aeneas' character change is complete by the beginning of Book VI; Pöschl, p. 37, places "the hero's emancipation from the burden of the past" in Books V-VIII; and Brooks Otis, _Virgil_ (Oxford: Oxford Univ. Press, 1964), p. 280, restricts Aeneas' change in character to Book VI alone.

4 Mario A. DiCesare, _The Altar and the City_ (New York: Columbia Univ. Press, 1974), suggests that the emotionally charged proper names in Hector's speech make Aeneas' response inevitable.

5 Otis, p. 244, finds fault with Venus' failure to use prophecy to motivate Aeneas, but I think she uses the arguments likeliest to be effective at this moment.

6 Austin, note to 2.781, glosses _Hesperiam_ as "in the West" and quotes Servius on the use of _Hesperia_ for Spain as well as Italy. Williams, note to 3.163, agrees that the name is ambiguous. R. B. Lloyd, "_Aeneid_ III: A New Approach," _American Journal of Philology_ 78 (1957), 134 and n. 9, cites four earlier critics who believe that Aeneas does not know where Hesperia is when Creusa names it. To assume otherwise is to make nonsense of Book III.

7 Williams, note to 3.107, ascribes the mistaken interpretation to the existence of two accounts of Troy's foundation, which are recorded in Servius' notes to 3.108 and 3.167. Here Anchises recalls the version in which Teucer comes to Troy before Dardanus does, but in the version evidently alluded to by the oracle Teucer left Crete after Dardanus arrived at Troy from Italy. According to the latter account, Teucer succeeded Dardanus as king.

8 W. S. Anderson, _The Art of the Aeneid_ (Englewood Cliffs, N.J.: Prentice-Hall, 1969), p. 28, agrees that Aeneas sees in the pictures the "sympathy which he has not often experienced since Troy's fall." Parry, p. 122, believes that Aeneas' pleasure is due rather to the transfiguring and redemptive power of art. W. R. Johnson, _Darkness Visible_ (Berkeley: Univ. of California Press, 1976), points out, p. 103,

that the pictures "are a kind of victory monument to Juno," and concludes, p. 104, that Aeneas "deludes himself into feeling heartened,"
unable to bear the weight of reality.

[9] Charles P. Segal, "Aeternum Per Saecula Nomen, The Golden Bough
and the Tragedy of History," Part 1, Arion, 4 (1965), 653, argues that
the consolation which the Sibyl offers Palinurus is both inappropriate
and inadequate to his situation and so fails "to mollify too much the
pain of his death."

[10] Johnson, pp. 82-84, compares this scene with its Homeric model,
in which the shade of Ajax refuses to speak with Odysseus.

[11] R. D. Williams, "The Sixth Book of the Aeneid," Greece and Rome,
2nd series, 11 (1964), 54, interprets the shades similarly.

[12] L. A. MacKay, "Three Levels of Meaning in Aeneid VI," Transactions
and Proceedings of the American Philological Association, 86 (1955),
185, discusses this function of the encounters with Dido and Deiphobus,
concluding that Aeneas' "sense of guilt" with regard to his actions
in Books II and IV "is dispelled by the recall and dismissal of these
experiences." Brooks Otis, "Three Problems of Aeneid 6," Transactions
and Proceedings of the American Philological Association, 90 (1959),
168, observes that Dido and Deiphobus appear exactly as they were at
the moment of death and argues that Aeneas "can only be liberated from
[the past's] hold by realizing that it is dead." Segal, p. 648, points
out that Palinurus was "intimately bound up with the years of effort
to reach the land of the future," and that "he points toward this
Italic future for which he steered."

[13] The structure of Anchises' revelation is analyzed in detail by
Robert J. Getty, "Romulus, Roma, and Augustus in the Sixth Book of
the Aeneid," Classical Philology, 45 (1950), 1; by George E. Duckworth,
"Animae Dimidium Meae: Two Poets of Rome," Transactions and Proceedings
of the American Philological Association, 87 (1956), 304-05 and note 79;
by R. D. Williams, "The Pageant of Roman Heroes--Aeneid 6.756-853," in
J. R. C. Martyn, ed., Cicero and Virgil (Amsterdam: Hakkert, 1972), p.
208; and in Austin's notes to 6.756-853. Getty sees six sections: kings
of Alba Longa (760-76); Romulus, Roma, and Augustus (777-90); Augustus'
exploits (791-807); Roman kings (808-18); Republican heroes (819-46);
and concluding message (847-53). Duckworth divides the prophecy into
two parts at line 807, subdividing the first half into the Alban kings
(760-76), Romulus (777-87), and Augustus (788-807); he subdivides the
second half into the same three sections Getty sees in lines 808-53.
Williams agrees with Duckworth both in seeing a two-part structure as
most important and, generally, in his subdivisions of the first part,
although he separates the last two lines (806-07) from the third sub-
division; he divides the second half into two main parts at the unfinished
line, 835, with lines 808-35 further subdivided into four sections and
lines 836-53 into two. Austin, like Getty, simply sees numerous short

sections; he groups Romulus with the Alban kings (760-87), keeps the Augustan material together (788-807), groups early kings with early Republicans (808-25), gives Caesar and Pompey a separate section (826-35), and separates the crowd of Roman conquerors (836-46) from the final message about Rome's achievements (847-53). Of all these schemes, the one devised by Williams comes closest to agreeing with my own reading of the prophecy.

[14] Of the four allusions to Troy and Trojans in Anchises' prophecy, three are genealogical. Procas of Alba Longa comes "of the Trojan race" (Troiana . . . gentis, 767), Romulus "of the blood of Assaracus" (Assaraci . . . sanguinis, 778), and the young Marcellus "of the Ilian race" (Iliaca . . . de gente, 875). Furthermore, by the time Anchises reaches the young Marcellus, other ancestry is equally important: the lad has "Latin forebears" (Latinos / . . . avos, 875-76) and inhabits "the land of Romulus" (Romula . . . / . . . tellus, 876-77). The fourth allusion to Troy occurs in Anchises' description of Rome's conquest of Greece as revenge for the Greek victory in the Trojan War (840).

[15] Jupiter's prophecy (1.267-77) is neatly structured in multiples of three: Aeneas will rule from Lavinium for three years, Ascanius will rule from Alba Longa for thirty years, and Aeneas' descendants will continue ruling from Alba Longa for three hundred years before Romulus founds Rome. Vergil achieved this neatness at the expense of fidelity to tradition; the traditional date of Rome's founding by Romulus is more than four hundred years later than that of Troy's fall.

[16] Kenneth Quinn, Virgil's Aeneid (London: Routledge & Kegan Paul, 1968), p. 172, claims that Vergil violates chronology in order to separate Augustus from "the other participants in the civil war, Julius Caesar and Pompey." Anderson, p. 61, suggests that Augustus appears between the kings and the Republicans since his position is "a blend of these two Roman traditions, fulfilling the best of both." Austin, in his note to lines 788ff., and Williams, "The Pageant of Roman Heroes," 208-09, agree that Vergil places Augustus next to Romulus to invite comparisons between the two, as I also argue.

[17] In his note to 6.808-09, Austin observes that the olive with which Numa is crowned is regularly a symbol of priesthood in the Aeneid; he cites 5.774, 7.414-18, 7.750-51. He also observes that Vergil repeats the phrase sacra ferens in describing Aeneas when the hero is about to sacrifice the white sow (8.85). These repetitions strengthen the probability that Vergil presents Numa as a role-model.

[18] Anchises had not followed a strictly chronological order in his survey of the Alban kings, either. He proceeded from Aeneas' son to three more distant descendants, one of them so far removed in time as Romulus' grandfather, before returning to Aeneas' grandson immediately before reaching Romulus. Anchises points out the following Republicans:

the Decii	4th and 3rd centuries B.C.
the Drusi	2nd and 1st centuries
Torquatus	1st century
Camillus	4th century
Caesar and Pompey	1st century
Mummius	2nd century
Aemilius Paullus	2nd century
Cato	2nd century
Cossus	5th century
the Gracchi	3rd and 2nd centuries
the Scipiones	3rd and 2nd centuries
Fabricius	3rd century
Serranus	2nd century
Fabius Maximus	3rd century
Marcellus (maior)	3rd century
Marcellus (minor)	1st century

Of the many reasons Vergil arranged these individuals and families in this order, attention to chronology is obviously not the most important principle.

[19] Williams, "The Pageant of Roman Heroes," pp. 212-13, reads the presentation of Brutus as almost unrelievedly negative and tentatively attributes the judgment he thinks Anchises passes on this Republican Brutus to Vergil's feelings toward his descendant, the slayer of Julius Caesar.

[20] Quinn, p. 49, faults Vergil for omitting Augustus from this consideration of participants in the civil war and for returning to the events of the preceding century at this point. Anderson, p. 63, believes that Vergil's "juxtaposition of the selfless Republican generals . . . and the self-seeking dynasts Caesar and Pompey" shows the poet's "mixed attitude of hate-love" toward warfare in general. Di Cesare, p. 117, agrees with Quinn that Vergil's return to earlier events constitutes a retreat from the substantive issues of the civil war. Williams, "The Pageant of Roman Heroes," pp. 214-15, notes the effect of Anchises' using the terms soter and gener, of his addressing the shades directly, of the alliteration in line 833, and of the unfinished line, 835. Although he does not state any overall conclusion explicitly, he seems to feel that the dominant mood of the passage is sorrow or pathos, not condemnation of either character by Anchises.

[21] Critics who agree, as I do, with Vergil's description of the achievements of Augustan Rome include Brooks Otis, "Virgil and Clio: A Consideration of Virgil's Relation to History," Phoenix, 20 (1966), 64; Williams, "The Sixth Book of the Aeneid," p. 61, and "The Pageant of Roman Heroes," p. 217; and Duckworth, p. 306. On the other hand, Quinn, p. 173, considers this passage a description of "the policy Augustus followed" in the civil war and regrets "the care, the embarrassment almost (betrayed by the false note struck in the final superbos),

with which Virgil voices even a veiled comment upon the civil war."
Since Anchises' address to Caesar and Pompey offers an unveiled comment
on the civil war, it hardly seems reasonable for Quinn to wrench this
passage into an inadequate treatment of the same concern. Di Cesare,
p. 119, argues that Anchises' views here cannot be identical with
Vergil's because Anchises only considers Greek and Roman characteristics instead of "total categories of reality." What other categories
of reality Vergil would have considered are not identified by Di Cesare.

[22] Johnson, p. 107, feels that the grief Anchises expresses at
Marcellus' untimely death "threatens to overwhelm the magnificence of
Roman achievement"; later, p. 110, he qualifies this statement: "The
pathos does not nullify the grandeur, but the grandeur does not redeem
the pathos." I see such comments as excessively pessimistic.

Chapter 2

THE EFFECT OF MERLIN'S PROPHECY ON BRITOMART

In his preface to The Faerie Queene, Spenser identified the hero
of Book III as "Britomartis a Lady knight."[1] Britomart's identification
as a lady knight joins her, as Hough observes, to "a long line of warrior
maidens who love and fight through the romantic epic."[2] Britomart
becomes a warrior maiden quite suddenly, as a young woman, whereas her
literary predecessors were warrior maids almost from infancy.[3] Her
change from one character type to another, from lovesick damsel to
warrior maid, received little critical attention until recently. Nine-
teenth- and early twentieth-century Spenserians concerned themselves
primarily with allegorical interpretation of the poem; once they had
equated Britomart with chastity, they concentrated on Spenser's definition of the virtue rather than on his presentation of its patron knight.
In the 1930s, when historical allegory replaced moral allegory as the
dominant mode of interpretation, critics generally read "Elizabeth" for
"Britomart" and proceeded to discuss Spenser's politics. With the
recent rise of psychological analysis in general and interest in sexual-
ity in particular, Britomart's character has received increasing attention.
Nevertheless, few critics have considered Britomart's change in character,
perhaps because Spenser's knights do not seem to develop in the ways
that characters develop in the novel, the chief model and source for
critics of narrative works since about 1800. Moreover, those who have

42

discussed Britmoart's transformation either fail to assess the effect
of Merlin's prophecy on Britomart, or misread the prophecy in ways which
limit the usefulness of their work.[4] In this chapter, therefore, I
shall discuss the process by which Britomart becomes a warrior maiden,
a process comparable to that by which Aeneas changes in the first half
of the Aeneid.

The traditional attributes of a warrior maiden are superior fighting ability, superlative beauty, and a commitment to either celibacy
or chastity. In Book III, Canto i, Britomart demonstrates her possession
of these traits. She unhorses Guyon for the first time in his life,
defeats five of the Redcross Knight's opponents in the time it takes
him to subdue one, and with his aid puts the same six knights to flight
in a later encounter (i.6-7, 28-29, 66). Although she uses her enchanted
spear on the first two occasions, she obtains her third victory with an
ordinary sword. Moreover, the possession of magical weapons traditionally reflects a knight's personal prowess rather than supplying it.
As for Britomart's beauty, Spenser compares her face when she raises
her visor to the moon breaking through a cloud (i.42-43). Her reactions
to the customs of Castle Joyous and to its mistress, Malecasta, reveal
her commitment to chastity (i.25, 40, 55). Our identification of her as
a typical warrior maid seems well-founded.

Yet in Spenser's account of her previous history, we discover not
a warrior maid, but a typical lovesick damsel. In a flashback (ii.17-52),
Spenser tells how Britomart saw Arthegall in a magic mirror and fell
in love with him. Ignorant of her malady's name and nature, she sighs,
weeps, and suffers alternately from the traditional insomnia and

nightmares of courtly love. Spenser repeatedly uses the conventional
love-imagery of wound and flame, thus reinforcing our identification of
Britomart at this stage of her life as a lovesick damsel. While
strength, independence, courage, and activity distinguish the warrior
maiden, weakness, reliance on others, fear, and passivity characterize
the lovesick damsel. The former acts alone or leads others into action,
as Britomart does in Canto i; the latter follows a confidante's advice
and depends on her for encouragement, as Britomart does throughout
Canto ii. Clearly, she has had to change radically, from suffering
damsel to active warrior.

But Spenser has not made it easy for the reader to see such a
radical change. In her own description of her upbringing, Britomart
pretends that she has always been a warrior maiden, and this description occurs before Spenser's account, which will contradict it:

> Faire Sir, I let you weete, that from the howre
> I taken was from nourses tender pap,
> I have beene trained up in warlike stowre,
> To tossen speare and shield, and to affrap
> The warlike ryder to his most mishap;
> Sithence I loathed have my life to lead,
> As Ladies wont, in pleasures wanton lap,
> To finger the fine needle and nyce thread;
> Me lever were with point of foemans speare be dead.
>
> (ii.6)

If Britomart's account here were truthful, one might expect her to
resume warlike activities after recovering from the physically debili-
tating stage of lovesickness. Yet in the flashback, it becomes clear
that Britomart had never received any knightly training before she fell
in love. When she has recovered from lovesickness, her nurse suggests
that she pretend to be a knight in order to seek her lover safely:

> That therefore nought our passage may empeach,
>   Let us in feigned armes our selves disguize,
>   And our weake hands (whom need new strength shall teach)
>   The dreadfull speare and shield to exercize:
>   Ne certes daughter that same warlike wize
>   I weene, would you misseeme; for ye bene tall,
>   And large of limbe, t'atchieve an hard emprize,
>   Ne ought ye want, but skill, which practize small
> Will bring, and shortly make you a mayd Martiall.
>   (iii.53)

Two possible explanations for this discrepancy exist. Either Spenser

altered his conception of Britomart's history and failed to amend one

passage, or Britomart lied to the Redcross Knight. Admittedly, other

discrepancies abound in the first cantos of Book III.[5]   The heading

to Canto i reads, "Duessaes traines and Malecastaes champions are

defaced," but Duessa does not appear in Book III at all. Then Spenser

calls the Redcross Knight "Guyon" in ii.4. Several lesser puzzles

allow explanations other than authorial carelessness, but obviously

Spenser did err on at least two occasions. Hence, the contradictions

in accounts of Britomart's upbringing could have resulted from a third

authorial error. However, the fact that the remainder of her speech

to the Redcross Knight consists of lies, which the reader is surely

expected to recognize as such, favors the other alternative. Britomart

slanders Arthegall repeatedly for the pleasure of hearing him defended

by her companion. Spenser comments on her having "missayd" and on her

slander's being "faind gainesay" (ii.9, 15). Inventing an autobiography

would apparently present no problem for Britomart. Having become a

knight in order to seek her lover, she disguises her gender whenever

possible in Faeryland, and at all times she hides her purpose in being

there.[6] A feigned account of her life-style in Britain would help to

hide the object of her quest from the Redcross Knight. Assuming that
Britomart lied on this occasion not only exonerates Spenser of large-
scale carelessness but also leaves the timing of Britomart's change in
characterization undisputed. She becomes the warrior maiden whom we
saw in Canto i only when she stops being the lovesick damsel whom we
meet in the flashback in Cantos ii and iii.

Very little happens between Britomart's falling in love and her
becoming a knight. Outwardly, her situation hardly changes. She does
not meet Arthegall, nor does he learn of her existence. Even his exact
location in Faeryland remains unknown, so that she searches for him
by riding about at random. Yet her attitude changes completely, from
despair so total that she nearly dies of it to confidence so certain
that she stays cheerful through many delays. Britomart's own actions
cannot account for her transformation, as she does not act on her own
initiative between looking in the mirror and leaving Britain. Instead,
she merely responds to what Glauce and Merlin say, and they share the
credit for her alteration.

Glauce has a smaller part to play than Merlin, but her success is
the prerequisite for his. She appoints herself Britomart's confidante,
a vital role; without Glauce's coaxing, Britomart would have kept her
love a secret and would have died of it. In order to obtain the princess' confidence, Glauce makes a vow, whose unforeseen consequence
triggers the plot. This vow, which is to help Britomart win her love,
presently forces Glauce to consult Merlin, her own efforts having failed.
Furthermore, Glauce frees Britomart from feeling ashamed of loving and
thereby prepares the princess to benefit from Merlin's instruction.

Many of Britomart's counterparts in classical and medieval literature also feel ashamed of loving. Their shame may be due to a conflict between the new love and an old loyalty, whether to family, to country, or to husband (living or dead); or it may be due to their having fallen in love with an inappropriate figure, such as a father, a brother, or an animal. Britomart is ashamed of loving an image rather than a real person. She calls her love "no usuall fire, no usuall rage" (ii.37) and is convinced that only death can put an end to her abnormal love-sickness (ii.39). Glauce immediately expresses her astonishment at such thinking: "what need ye be dismayd, / Or why make ye such Monster of your mind?" (ii.40). Britomart's passion sounds like a normal case of love at first sight to her old nurse:

> But this affection nothing straunge I find:
> For who with reason can you aye reprove,
> To love the semblant pleasing most your mind,
> And yield your heart, whence ye cannot remove?
>
> (ii.40)

To reassure Britomart further, Glauce compares her choice with the incestuous or bestial lovers chosen by Myrrhe, Biblis, and Pasiphaë (ii.41). Despite the "strange beginning" of Britomart's desire, to Glauce it "certes seemes bestowed not amis" (ii.42). Britomart fully accepts Glauce's judgment of her morality, conceding that "my love be not so lewdly bent, / As those ye blame" (ii.43).[7]

Britomart has also accepted Glauce's belief that Arthegall really exists. She had originally thought her vision an illusion: "Nor man it is, nor other living wight" (ii.38). Yet faith in his reality does not end her despair, for she deems it hopeless to "love a shade, the bodie farre exild" (ii.44), as Narcissus did. Glauce points out that

Narcissus loved his own shadow, while Britomart loves "the shadow of
a warlike knight," and that magic may tell them where to find Arthegall
(ii.45). These assurances cheer Britomart enough for her to sleep a
little. Thus Glauce has not only dispelled the princess' shame but
has also given her some hope.

Having freed Britomart wholly from her self-destructive sense of
shame and partially from her despair, Glauce proceeds to offer the
princess two kinds of assistance. Because it would be difficult to find
the knight in question, Glauce advises Britomart to reason herself out
of love and promises to aid that endeavor with spells and charms.
Should this joint attempt fail, she promises to help Britomart locate
her lover:

> But if the passion mayster thy fraile might,
> So that needs love or death must be thy lot,
> Then I avowe to thee, by wrong or right
> To compasse thy desire, and find that loved knight.
> (ii.46)

Not surprisingly, the spells and charms have no effect, and the princess'
physical decline continues. Glauce admits defeat and decides to consult
Merlin, since he had made the magic mirror in which Britomart saw
Arthegall.

When Glauce and Britomart reach Merlin's cave, the princess temporarily takes the lead:

> They here ariving, staid a while without,
>   Ne durst adventure rashly in to wend,
>   But of their first intent gan make new dout
>   For dread of daunger, which it might portend:
>   Untill the hardie Mayd (with love to frend)
>   First entering, the dreadfull Mage there found
>   Deepe busied bout worke of wondrous end,
>   And writing strange characters in the ground,
> With which the stubborn feends he to his service bound.
> (iii.14)

Britomart proves braver than Glauce because love can have strengthening
as well as weakening effects. Spenser reminded the readers of that
fact when he opened Canto iii with a hymn to love, "Whence spring all
noble deeds and never dying fame" (iii.1), and here we see the first
evidence of love's ennobling Britomart. She will become a warrior
maid for the sake of love, just as she has been on the verge of death
on its account, and this act of courage, though minor, foreshadows her
transformation. Nevertheless, her hardiness deserts her again once
she faces Merlin. Glauce speaks for her during the first part of their
visit, and Britomart blushes in silence when Merlin addresses her.

Merlin's first words to Britomart begin correcting a misconception
that she and Glauce shared, their belief that chance rather than providence rules the world. Britomart saw Arthegall's image because she
wondered "Whom fortune for her husband would allot" (ii.23), and she
laments her "misfortune," "hard fortune," and "wicked fortune" thereafter (ii.38, 39, 44). Glauce not only speaks of "better fortune"
(ii.45), but also refers to Cupid as "That blinded God, which hath ye
blindly smit" (ii.35), as if Britomart had fallen in love by accident.
Merlin, however, introduces the concept of fate when he first greets
Britomart:

> Ne ye faire Britomartis, thus arayd,
> More hidden are, then Sunne in cloudy vele;
> Whom thy good fortune, having fate obayd,
> Hath hither brought, for succour to appele;
> The which the powres to thee are pleased to revele.
> (iii.19)

In the hierarchy Merlin's speech implies, fate outranks fortune. What
appears to mortals as good or bad luck results from their acting in
accord with or in opposition to the decrees of fate. In later lines,

Merlin will use "heavenly destiny" and "eternall providence" as synonyms
for "fate," thus making it clear that he understands fate to be the
will of God. According to Merlin, God had arranged for Britomart to
see Arthegall's image:[8]

> It was not, Britomart, thy wandring eye,
>   Glauncing unwares in charmed looking glas,
> But the streight course of heavenly destiny,
> Led with eternall providence, that has
> Guided thy glaunce, to bring his will to pas.
>   (iii.24)

The magician's conclusion ("Therefore submit thy wayes unto his will,"
iii.24) has the force of a religious commandment; Britomart must cease
lamenting the love God has chosen for her. Merlin will reinforce this
lesson in his prophecy by showing Britomart how historical events which
seem to result from chance actually form part of God's plan for British
history.

The discovery that God has a plan for an individual's life can
lead to thinking that the individual need not act at all, but should
merely accept whatever occurs. Glauce, thinking in just such a fashion,
asks Merlin why Britomart should seek for Arthegall, since they are
fated to meet and marry. His response clarifies the role individuals
play in human history:

> Indeed the fates are firme,
> And may not shrinck, though all the world do shake:
> Yet ought mens good endevours them confirme,
> And guide the heavenly causes to their constant terme.
>   (iii.25)

"Good endevours" help bring God's will to pass, but it would come to
fulfillment even if men tried to prevent it. Yet each person remains
free to choose whether to help or to hinder, and his choice becomes the
means by which events proceed to their destined end. Since the individual

guides the earthly progress of God's plan just as much as God guides
the individual, Britomart must transform herself from a passive to an
active character, a doer of deeds and not merely a hearer of words.[9]

Nevertheless, Britomart also needs to listen to Merlin's advice,
to understand her passion before she takes action. He has already
explained to her the purpose of her suffering:

> Most noble Virgin, that by fatall lore
> Hast learn'd to love, let no whit thee dismay
> The hard begin, that meets thee in the dore,
> And with sharpe fits thy tender hart oppresseth sore.
>
> For so must all things excellent begin,
> And eke enrooted deepe must be that Tree,
> Whose big embodied braunches shall not lin,
> Till they to heavens hight forth stretched bee.
>
> (iii.21-22)

Glauce had called love a "deepe engraffed ill" (iii.18), as if it
were artificially grafted onto Britomart, but Merlin's image corrects
Glauce's by depicting love as a natural growth. The tree simultaneously
represents Britomart's love, which needed to take root in her before
it could bear fruit, and the family tree of her descendants, the "big
embodied braunches."[10] The image therefore serves as a transition
from her individual fate to the future generations which depend on her
for their existence:

> For from thy wombe a famous Progenie
> Shall spring, out of the auncient Trojan blood,
> Which shall revive the sleeping memorie
> Of those same antique Peres, the heavens brood,
> Which Greeke and Asian rivers stained with their blood.
>
> (iii.22)

Britomart will transmit to her descendants her own heritage of Trojan
valor. Their destiny, to revive the classical heroes' forgotten
virtues, demands their descent from that "heavenly brood." Britomart's

love for Arthegall connects the past to the future and thereby establishes continuity into a world of violent change.

Nevertheless, the world will continue violent, as Merlin acknowledges by presenting Britomart's descendants primarily in terms of their military deeds:

> Renowmed kings, and sacred Emperours,
>   Thy fruitfull Ofspring, shall from thee descend;
> Brave Captaines, and most mighty warriours,
>   That shall their conquests through all lands extend,
>   And their decayed kingdomes shall amend:
> The feeble Britons, broken with long warre,
>   They shall upreare, and mightily defend
>   Against their forrein foe, that comes from farre,
> Till universall peace compound all civill jarre.
>
> (iii.23)

This brief account proceeds from strength to weakness and back to strength again. Had the generations after Britomart consisted solely of "Renowmed kings," presumably their kingdoms would never have "decayed." More explicitly, Merlin admits that "long warre" will weaken the British people. He implies that they will fight not only "Against their forrein foe," but also among themselves, in "civill jarre." Still, he emphasizes not their decline but their recovery, the amendment of their kingdoms, the restoration of their strength, and their eventual enjoyment of "universall peace."[11] This pattern of a happy resolution of long-lasting difficulties applies to Britomart's love as well as to the history of her offspring. Just as the Britons' domestic and foreign wars will give way to universal concord, so Britomart's emotional distress and the physical perils of her quest will end in her fruitful marriage.

Merlin's speech (iii.21-24) has given Britomart a general understanding of the role her love plays in the divine plan, but it has not

provided any immediately useful information. Glauce therefore demands
specific advice: "What meanes shall she out seeke, or what wayes take? /
How shall she know, how shall she find the man?" (iii.25). In response,
Merlin identifies Arthegall as "The man whom heavens have ordaynd to
bee / The spouse of Britomart" (iii.26), as if his importance, like
hers, lay primarily in their marriage. Kidnapped in infancy, Arthegall
lives in Faeryland, ignorant of his human nature and his British origin.
Yet he belongs to Cornwall's ruling family, and Britomart must bring
him back to strengthen the British defence against the Saxons.[12] Merlin
does not say how to accomplish this task, nor does he answer any of
Glauce's questions. Instead, he proceeds to predict the course of
British history for centuries to come.

By the beginning of Merlin's historical prophecy, Britomart has
acquired much of the knowledge she lacked in Canto ii. Before consulting Merlin, she still feared that Arthegall would prove unattainable,
despite Glauce's repeated assurances that they could find him. Although
her nurse had dispelled her most serious misgivings about her love,
she did not understand its true nature completely. Finally, she had
no comprehension of God's interest in her loving and marrying Arthegall.
Merlin's first speeches have convinced Britomart that she will find
Arthegall, explained the nature and purpose of her love, and revealed
that God has chosen this love for her. Aeneas had reached a similar
point by the time the Review of Heroes begins in _Aeneid_ VI. In Books
I-IV, he had feared that his new home would prove unattainable, despite
multiple prophecies which assured him he would find it. Although those
prophecies had told him much about his task, he did not yet comprehend

its true nature fully. Finally, he had still not realized that the gods
had destined him to complete his task. Mercury's appearance to Aeneas
at Carthage had the same effects on him as Merlin's first speeches had
on Britomart. Mercury convinced Aeneas that he would find his new
home, suggested that it would be in name and nature different from
Aeneas' previous expectations, and revealed the extent of the gods'
interest in Aeneas' success. As we have already seen, Anchises' revelation of Roman history completed the process of inspiring and instructing
Aeneas; Merlin's prediction of British history will complete an analogous process for Britomart.

Merlin's historical prophecy divides into two sections. The
first section provides a concise but thorough account of the period
from Arthegall's return from Faeryland through Cadwallader's exile to
Armorica (iii.28-42). After Britomart responds to this section and
asks Merlin to continue, he gives an extremely abridged account of
the eight hundred years following Cadwallader's exile, ending with the
reign of Elizabeth (iii.43-49). The first section teaches Britomart
that good and bad fortune alternate arbitrarily and that divine providence controls human history despite the apparent vagaries of fortune.
Thus it completes her education in indifference toward worldly success
and failure and in trust in God's mysterious ways. The second section
inspires her by revealing that neither her descendants nor the valor
and virtue she will bequeath them will die out and that the continuity
of her line, her love, and her courage will eventually bring Britain
peace. Both the instruction and the inspiration offered by Merlin
encourage Britomart to become an active character rather than a passive

one, motivated by love to do great deeds rather than driven by love
to suffer great pains.

The events Merlin narrates in the first section show that neither
good fortune nor bad lasts long. Britomart will be widowed when
Arthegall dies young, "Too rathe cut off by practise criminall / Of
secret foes" (iii.28). Their son will defeat the Mercians twice and
then make peace with them, but his happiness appears uncertain thereafter: "And if he then with victorie can lin, / He shall his dayes
with peace bring to his earthly In" (iii.30; emphasis added). His son
Vortipore will enjoy a few victories, "But at the last to th'impor-
tunity / Of froward fortune shall be forst to yield" (iii.31).
Vortipore's son Malgo will avenge him and will proceed to great triumphs.
In him the personal appearance of the ancient heroes will live again,
and he will restore the classical boundaries of Britannia:

> Behold the man, and tell me Britomart,
>   If ay more goodly creature thou didst see;
>   How like a Gyaunt in each manly part
>   Beares he himselfe with portly majestee,
>   That one of th'old Heroes seemes to bee:
>   He the six Islands, comprovinciall
>   In auncient times unto great Britainee,
>   Shall to the same reduce, and to him call
> Their sundry kings to do their homage severall.
>   (iii.32)

Malgo's success will not outlast him, though; in his son Careticus'
time, Norse invaders will utterly devastate Britain. The Saxon
Etheldred will defeat the remaining Britons twice before the wheel turns
again. Then Cadwan, Careticus' successor, will slaughter the Saxons in
a third encounter. His heir, Cadwallin, will slay Etheldred's son
and grandsons and will not lose any battle which he conducts in person.

Nevertheless, the British kingdom will end with his death. His son Cadwallader will die in exile, never having ruled his people. Thus victory will alternate with defeat from one generation to the next, or even within a single reign.

Merlin does not correlate the success or failure of these kings with their virtues or vices. On the contrary, he describes all the Britons before Cadwallin's time as morally superior to their enemies.[13] His comparison of Arthegall's son to a lion derives from Biblical prophecies of the Lion of Judah, and therefore sanctifies the British king. In contrast, his prediction that Gormond, "Like a swift Otter, fell through emptinesse, / Shall overswim the sea" (iii.33) makes the Norse leader seem bestial.[14] The British Cadwan wages war out of compassion, "pittying his peoples ill," whereas Etheldred fights "Serving th'ambitious will of Augustine," a less laudable motive (iii.35). Merlin describes the Britons whom Etheldred kills as "massacred Martyrs," thus implying that God prefers the British people to their opponents (iii.35). The situation changes abruptly, however, when Cadwallin forfeits God's favor.

Cadwallin begins well, defeating Etheldred's son, Edwin, and executing a wicked enchanter. In a later battle, he slays Edwin's twin sons and two Scottish kings. When another enemy, Penda, surrenders voluntarily, Cadwallin orders him to subdue his fellow-Saxons:

> He marching forth with fury insolent
> Against the good king Oswald, who indewd
> With heavenly powre, and by Angels reskewd,
> All holding crosses in their hands on hye,
> Shall him defeate withouten bloud imbrewd.
>
> (iii.38)

Oswald clearly enjoys God's favor, but the British king somehow fails

to recognize that fact:

> Whereat Cadwallin wroth, shall forth issew,
> And an huge hoste into Northumber lead,
> With which he godly Oswald shall subdew,
> And crowne with martyrdome his sacred head.
>
> (iii.39)

Later, Penda dies treacherously attacking Oswald's brother, to whom

Cadwallin had promised peace in exchange for tribute. For Cadwallin

to ally himself with a traitor like Penda against a saint like Oswald

indicates that he cannot distinguish between good and evil--at least,

among Saxons. God's displeasure takes the form of "plagues and murrins

pestilent" (iii.40), as it had in Moses' time, but these plagues result

in the enslavement of a chosen people.[15] When "the good Cadwallader"

(iii.40) plans to return to Britain after eight years of pestilence, he

> Shalbe by vision staid from his intent:
> For th'heavens have decreed, to displace
> The Britons, for their sinnes dew punishment,
> And to the Saxons over-give their government.
>
> (iii.41)

Unlike Cadwallin, Cadwallader does not strive against the manifest will

of God, and so the British kingdom comes to an end.

Merlin has shaped his material up to this point to illustrate two

lessons. The first is that neither good fortune nor bad lasts long.

Traditionally, examples of fortune's arbitrary reversals teach men not

to take their temporal gains and losses too seriously. Men should

neither despair in defeat nor rejoice unduly in victory. The question

then arises as to whether an individual should care about anything.

Merlin's second lesson, that fate decrees the direction of history

despite the vagaries of fortune,[16] answers this question. As a whole,

then, the first section of his prophecy displays in practice the relationship between fortune and fate which he had previously explained
in theory. Britomart needs to learn these lessons in order to endure
the dangers and distresses of her quest. She must believe that she
will complete the quest successfully and that its successful completion
will recompense her for its pains. Therefore, Merlin teaches her to
trust in the heavenly guidance of historical events and shows her that
her marriage to Arthegall has consequences far greater than her own
brief happiness.

Spenser manipulated the chronicle accounts considerably to produce
his tidy alternation of victory and defeat and to provide sufficient
evidence of God's guiding hand. Because he had invented Britomart,
she could proceed from sorrow without contradicting any records. The
next two generations posed problems, however. Although Spenser never
names the son whom Britomart bears to Arthegall, most scholars identify
him with the chronicles' Aurelius Conanus.[17] The line of succession
supports such an identification: Arthegall's son takes the crown from
Constantius and leaves it to his son Vortipore. Yet Aurelius Conanus
enjoys no military triumphs, and Arthegall's son wins a war with Mercia,
a war which Spenser had to invent. This victory provides a happy contrast to Arthegall's untimely death. In order to continue the pattern
of alternating success and failure, Spenser ascribed to Vortipore a
military defeat for which he had no historical authority. Thereafter
the chronicles supplied a series of alternately triumphant and disastrous
reigns. All the changes Spenser made in this early portion of the
prophecy illustrate the desired lesson, that reversals of fortune occur

in an apparently arbitrary manner.

In the later portion of the prophecy, Spenser introduced one wholly original incident, Penda's bloodless defeat by an army of angels with crosses in their hands. According to the chronicles, Penda loses a battle to Oswald in the ordinary fashion, but Cadwallin comes to his aid and Penda kills Oswald in the ensuing encounter.[18] This version gives Cadwallin no indication of God's favor towards Oswald and thus no opportunity to flout the will of God. Spenser utterly transforms the meaning of these events by introducing Oswald's miraculous victory. The poetic Cadwallin must choose whether or not to heed the supernatural warning, and his wrong choice brings down the wrath of God on the British people. Spenser's version thus shows providence determining the direction of history much more actively than the chronicles imply. Like the changes discussed earlier, this alteration in the chronicle material illustrates a lesson Britomart needs to learn.

Yet Britomart can hardly consider the results of divine intervention a cheerful prospect. If the consequences of her marriage to Arthegall consist of their descendants' forfeiting the kingdom, she might even wonder whether they should marry. Merlin describes the Britons' enslavement in the most dismal terms:[19]

> Then woe, and woe, and everlasting woe,
>   Be to the Briton babe, that shalbe borne,
>   To live in thraldome of his fathers foe;
>   Late King, now captive, late Lord, now forlorne,
>   The worlds reproch, the cruell victours scorne,
>   Banisht from Princely bowre to wastfull wood:
>   O who shall helpe me to lament, and mourne
>   The royall seed, the antique Trojan blood,
> Whose Empire lenger here, then ever any stood.
>   (iii.42)

Although Britomart fully shares Merlin's feelings, she questions his
calling their people's sorrow "everlasting":

> The Damzell was full deepe empassioned,
>   Both for his griefe, and for her peoples sake,
> Whose future woes so plaine he fashioned,
> And sighing sore, at length him thus bespake;
> Ah but will heavens fury never slake,
> Nor vengeaunce huge relent it selfe at last?
> Will not long misery late mercy make,
> But shall their name for ever be defast,
> And quite from of the earth their memory be rast?
>
> (iii.43)

Britomart has not previously spoken to Merlin, but her question indicates that she has profited from his instruction. She does not lament
the Britons' misfortune or ill-luck. Instead, she accepts their plight
as both destined and deserved, only questioning whether heaven will
administer justice without mercy, whether suffering will fail to evoke
pity at last. Evidently Britomart has learned both to acknowledge the
power of providence and to remain hopeful in unhappy circumstances.

Merlin assures her that she has not wasted her hope. The Britons'
thralldom will last for a "just revolution" of eight hundred years,
"Ere they to former rule restor'd shalbee" (iii.44). The magician
mentions only three Britons during that period, each of whom will
revive some aspect of British greatness.[20] In the ninth century, the
Saxon kings will seek Rhodoricke's friendship out of respect for his
personal bravery. Howell Dha will teach his people to honor justice
and truth, even in the savage state to which the Saxons will have
reduced them by the tenth century. Two hundred years later, Griffyth
Conan will renew the "old sparkes" of courage among the Britons so
thoroughly "that his foes shall feare, / Least backe againe the kingdome

he from them should beare" (iii.45). The valor and virtue of their

Trojan ancestors will live on in these heroic leaders of the British

people, even in slavery. Without such continuity, no restoration of

the British kingdom could occur.

Merlin also predicts the Danish invasions and the Norman conquest.

Because the Saxons will have "ruled wickedly," the Danes will "tread

downe the victours surquedry" (iii.46). God will use the Danes to

punish the Saxons, just as He used the Saxons to punish the Britons.

Then the Norman conqueror "from the Daniske Tyrants head shall rend /

Th'usurped crowne" and shall oppress all three peoples equally (iii.47).

These violent upheavals make a peaceful future possible, as each new

tyranny forces the previous victors to mingle with those they vanquished.

By describing these invaders as beasts, Merlin implies that they will

not make any other positive contribution:[21]

> There shall a Raven far from rising Sunne,
> With his wide wings upon them fiercely fly,
> And bid his faithlesse chickens overronne
> The fruitfull plaines. . . .
>
> (iii.46)

> There shall a Lyon from the sea-bord wood
> Of Neustria come roring, with a crew
> Of hungry whelpes, his battailous bold brood,
> Whose clawes were newly dipt in cruddy blood.
>
> (iii.47)

Such language suggests that any virtue to appear later must derive

from the British inheritance.

Having skimmed over eight hundred years of history, Merlin quickly

reaches the accession of Henry VII, an event he describes metaphorically:

> Tho when the terme is full accomplishid,
> There shall a sparke of fire, which hath long-white
> Bene in his ashes raked up, and hid,

> Be freshly kindled in the fruitfull Ile
> Of Mona, where it lurked in exile;
> Which shall breake forth into bright burning flame,
> And reach into the house, that beares the stile
> Of royall majesty and soveraigne name;
> So shall the Briton bloud their crowne againe reclame.
>   (iii.48)

Fire commonly represents both love and courage, qualities necessary for the restoration of a British monarchy.[22] Love kindles desire and thereby causes fruitfulness; to reclaim the throne requires courage. Henry Tudor will exist because of generations of loving marriages, and he will inherit the brave dispositions of his ancestors. The metaphor as a whole depicts the continuity of the royal family. Like a carefully banked fire, it has never died out, and oppression has not extinguished the valor of its members. In Britomart, as in her distant descendant, the spark of love will ignite the flame of courage, and the result in both cases will be the restoration of the greatness of the British people.

The deeds of Arthegall and Britomart will only temporarily improve their people's lot, but the accession of the Tudors will bring about perpetual concord:

> Thenceforth eternall union shall be made
>   Betweene the nations different afore,
> And sacred Peace shall lovingly perswade
>   The warlike minds, to learne her goodly lore,
>   And civile armes to exercise no more:
> Then shall a royall virgin raine, which shall
>   Stretch her white rod over the Belgicke shore,
>   And the great Castle smite so sore with all,
> That it shall make him shake and shortly learne to fall.
>   (iii.49)

At last the races of Britain will become one and civil wars will cease.[23] Earlier events have anticipated such a union but failed to

establish it eternally: Arthegall's son made a "faire accordaunce"
with the Mercians (iii.30); Malgo temporarily unified the British
Isles (iii.32). Love will bring permanent harmony out of the long
discord of British history, just as it will resolve the strife between
Britomart and Arthegall in order to bring about their own eternal union.
In Merlin's prophecy, Britain's internal peace permits the virgin queen
to protect neighboring countries and punish external foes.[24] Likewise, once Britomart and Arthegall have attained domestic concord,
they will defend their people against foreign invaders in a just war.
Love causes peace within a family or a realm, but leads to strength
and courage in dealings with the enemies of that family or that realm.

The second section of Merlin's prophecy completes Britomart's
education in hope by giving her something to hope for. She learns
of the continuity of virtue and valor in the unbroken line of her
descendants, and she discovers that the love and courage she possesses
will not only restore her offspring to the throne but will also bring
about an era of internal peace and external power for her homeland.
This vision of the distant future heartens her in preparation for the
difficulties of her quest. By telling Britomart about the consequences
of her marriage, Merlin identifies her love for Britain and for the
British people with her love for Arthegall. Since her quest will
affect the course of history, it merits more effort than one involving
merely personal happiness. Furthermore, the descendants whom Merlin
describes act out of the virtues she will transmit to them and thereby
show her how to realize her own potential for action. Everything Merlin
says encourages Britomart to exchange passivity for activity. Having

taught her earlier to disregard fleeting fortune and trust in eternal providence, he finally displays to her the right relationship between passion and action, with Rhodoricke, Howell Dha, Griffyth Conan, Henry VII, and Elizabeth as exemplars of love and courage used to fulfill the decrees of fate.

Spenser did not need to alter the chronicle material for this section of Merlin's prophecy. He did abridge it drastically, so that Britomart seems closer to the Tudors than a fuller account would permit.[25] Economically, each of the three Welsh princes he picks exemplifies an aspect of his theme: friendship between two races, the continuity of classical virtues, courage capable of resuming power. He used the tradition of identifying rulers by their heraldic devices to make the Danes and the Normans seem bestial and thus morally inferior to their British subjects. Finally, he employed the metaphorical style found in the chronicles' historical prophecies to depict Henry VII's accession as a natural physical process. The internal audience of Merlin's prophecy, which consists of Glauce and Britomart, need not know about Bosworth Field; the external audience, which includes Elizabeth, does not want a reminder of it. These ways of presenting his historical material serve two purposes: they enable Spenser to give his characters an inspiring vision of the distant future, and they prevent his giving his readers any political offense.

Ending the prophecy posed problems for Spenser with regard to both audiences. He dared not hint at events after Elizabeth's death, lest he seem to advise her about the succession. For that matter, he could not safely predict any event later than the time at which he wrote.

On the other hand, Britomart could easily ask for more information about this other royal maiden or about the continuation of her descendants' line. Spenser prevents such questions within the poem without offending anyone outside the poem:

> But yet the end is not. There Merlin stayd,
>   As overcomen of the spirites powre,
>   Or other ghastly spectacle dismayd,
>   That secretly he saw, yet note discoure;
>   Which suddein fit, and halfe extatick stoure
>   When the two fearefull women saw, they grew
>   Greatly confused in behavioure;
>   At last the fury past, to former hew
> Hee turnd againe, and chearefull looks as earst did shew.
>   (iii.50)

Spenser offers two explanations for Merlin's abrupt silence.[26] He may have been merely "overcomen of the spirites powre," unable to speak due to an involuntary deepening of his prophetic trance. Divine or demonic possession makes prophecy possible, but it can also cause fits of abstraction, unintelligible speech, and other symptoms. The terms "suddeine fit," "halfe extactick stoure," and "fury" all indicate that the spirit possessing Merlin overpowers him briefly. However, Spenser has also said that Merlin may have become "dismayd" at some "ghastly spectacle." Certainly the last two lines of the stanza imply that his looks were not cheerful during this episode. Although Spenser has not suggested what sort of spectacle might have dismayed Merlin, the Elizabethan reader could imagine a variety of acceptable possibilities: renewed continental warfare, for example, or the queen's death. In the latter case, Merlin's dismay would seem complimentary to Elizabeth. Moreover, whatever causes the magician's alteration in manner effectively prevents Glauce and Britomart from questioning him further.

Most importantly, Merlin's mysterious and disturbing behavior
does not nullify the positive effect his prophecy has had on Britomart.
She and Glauce, "both conceiving hope of comfort glad, / With lighter
hearts unto their home retird" (iii.51). Britomart has thoroughly
learned to trust in divine providence despite arbitrary reversals
of fortune and in the ability of valor and virtue to establish peace.
Therefore, she does not let Merlin's apparent dismay continue troubling
her once he recovers. In _Aeneid_ VI, Anchises' lament for young
Marcellus similarly does not detract from the positive effect which
the Review of Heroes has had on Aeneas, who has learned that Augustus
will establish peace and that Rome's achievements will be worth their
cost. Indeed, the two historical prophecies resemble each other in
many ways. The first half of Anchises' revelation, like the second
section of Merlin's, condenses a vast period of history in order to
reach the poet's own ruler. These sections of the prophecies serve
primarily to inspire the listening hero and heroine, dispelling their
doubts and fears, providing them with role models from among their
own descendants, and showing them the concord which their people
will eventually enjoy. The second half of Anchises' prophecy, like
the first section of Merlin's, recounts the deeds (mostly military)
of a large number of historical figures. These sections primarily
educate the listening characters, teaching them to judge events not
by the joy or sorrow immediately produced but by the causes and long-
term consequences involved. Vergil departs from chronological order
to juxtapose tragic patriots and happy ones, self-serving generals
and self-sacrificing ones, so that Aeneas may learn that service to

Rome, not personal happiness, matters most. Likewise, Spenser departs
from historical tradition so that Britomart may learn that obedience
to God, not personal success, matters most. Rome's great civilizing
mission and the divine plan for British history do not differ as much
as they might appear to at first glance; Anchises' concluding statement that Rome will "wear down the proud with war" (debellare superbos,
Aen. 6.853) would surely seem to Spenser a good description of the
actions which Merlin's "royall virgin" takes toward "the great
Castle" (iii.49). Finally, the effects the prophecies have on Aeneas
and Britomart are analogous. Both characters needed to acquire hope
in order to act rather than suffer, knowledge in order to act rightly,
and an understanding of the purpose their actions would serve in
order to persevere despite future difficulties. The historical predictions, although they both end somberly, give Aeneas and Britomart
the necessary hope, knowledge, and understanding and thus complete
the process of committing them to cooperation with their destinies.

Upon Britomart's return home, she and Glauce consider how to
begin cooperating with her fate. For a princess to travel to another
country in search of a knight poses certain tactical problems. Glauce
suggests that Britomart become a warrior maid and cites precedents
among the princess' ancestors for such behavior:

> The bold Bunduca, whose victorious
> Exploits made Rome to quake, stout Guendolen,
> Renowmed Martia, and redoubted Emmilen.
>
> (iii.54)

Britomart undoubtedly has long known her own family history, so she
would recognize these examples,[27] to which the nurse adds Angela, a

Saxon queen from their own time. Angela leads her people in battle and
they call themselves Angles for love of her. Glauce concludes, "Therefore faire Infant her ensample make / Unto thyselfe, and equall
courage to thee take" (iii.56). Britomart does so without delay:

> Her harty words so deepe into the mynd
>   Of the young Damzell sunke, that great desire
>   Of warlike armes in her forthwith they tynd,
>   And generous stout courage did inspire,
>   That she resolv'd, unweeting to her Sire,
>   Advent'rous knighthood on her selfe to don,
>   And counseld with her Nourse, her Maides attire
>   To turn into a massy habergeon,
> And bad her all things put in readinesse anon.
>   (iii.57)

Stanza 56 constitutes the last occasion on which Glauce addresses
Britomart as a nurse would a child or a confidante would a lovesick
heroine. Spenser's verbs in stanza 57 trace Britomart's rapid change
from follower to leader: she makes a resolution, takes counsel with
Glauce as a ruler does with a minister, and bids Glauce procure what
they have agreed she will need for her resolved course of action.

Since some recently captured Saxon supplies included a suit of
Angela's armor, Britomart has no trouble outfitting herself. Armed
with the enchanted spear and the shield of a former British king,
and with Glauce as her squire, she rides forth to find Arthegall,
looking the complete warrior maid. So dressed, Britomart represents
the resolution of opposites: British in person, Saxon in armor; a
lover in purpose, a warrior in appearance and behavior. She thus
symbolizes the eventual union of her people with Angela's and the
marital union in which she and Arthegall will become one. As her
mission has both national and personal consequences, so she becomes

an emblem of both historical and individual processes. Undoubtedly
Spenser makes Britomart a symbol of concord partly to reinforce the
parallel between her and Queen Elizabeth, already suggested by
Britomart's identity as the patron of chastity. Elizabeth Tudor
represented not only the union of Welsh and English royal blood, but
also the union of the houses of York and Lancaster. She symbolized
the resolution of the civil wars as visibly as did the Tudor rose,
a hybrid of red and white. Yet even if Spenser had not had political
reasons to give Britomart her emblematic coat of mail, the literary
reasons would have sufficed.[28] For Britomart changes character from
the typical lovesick damsel to the warrior maid by resolving the
discord between passion and action within herself. She exhibits both
love and courage, the gifts of Venus and Mars, without subordinating
either one to the other. Glauce made her unashamed of loving in
Canto ii; in Canto iii, Merlin showed her the role her love played
in God's plans for her people and thereby gave her the courage to act.
Thanks to his explanation of fate and fortune and his historical
prophecy, Britomart rides forth toward Faeryland with her internal
conflicts as fully resolved as her external roles.

Notes

[1] "A letter of the authors expounding his whole intention in the course of this worke," Roche, F.Q., p. 16.

[2] Graham Hough, "The Allegory of The Faerie Queene," in The Prince of Poets, ed. John R. Elliott, Jr. (New York: New York University Press, 1968), p. 218.

[3] Most classical warrior maidens, such as Hippolyte and Penthesilea, were Amazons, born and raised in a community of women warriors. Vergil's Camilla, who appears in Aeneid VII and XI, is an exception: she comes from a more normal community and leads a primarily masculine army, its only other warrior maids her own bodyguard. She is the ultimate source for such figures as Marfisa and Bradamante in Ariosto's Orlando Furioso and Clorinda in Tasso's Gerusalemme Liberata. In all of these cases, the maiden had been trained in arms as long as she could remember, unlike Britomart.

[4] Thomas P. Roche, Jr., The Kindly Flame (Princeton: Princeton Univ. Press, 1964), in an otherwise illuminating study of Books III and IV, does not discuss either Britomart's change of character type or any of Merlin's speeches. Kathleen Williams, Spenser's Faerie Queene (London: Routledge & Kegan Paul, 1966), pp. 93-95, provides a brief but excellent discussion of Glauce's interaction with Britomart and of Merlin's explanation of divinely willed fate, but analyzes only a few stanzas in Merlin's prophecy and so sees only one of its themes, that of divine guidance of human history. Harry Berger, Jr., "The Structure of Merlin's Chronicle in The Faerie Queene 3 (iii)," Studies in English Literature, 9 (1969), 39-51, also does a generally good job of explicating Merlin's speech about divinely willed fate, but he insists on reading the prophecy pessimistically in three ways: because he finds all military activity negative, he condemns many of Britomart's valiant descendants for what he calls in the case of her son a "sort of virtue [which] seems to us dated if not suspect" (43); he feels that the prophecy emphasizes the inevitable recurrence of violence throughout human history; and he believes that the Tudor establishment of national unity represents not so much the resoration of British rule as the replacement of primitive ethnic alignments with complex political ones, thus rendering the Britons' simple virtues permanently useless. These interpretations cannot account for the effect Merlin's prophecy has on Britomart, but Berger does not discuss that issue. Angus Fletcher, The Prophetic Moment (Chicago: Univ. of Chicago Press, 1971), pp. 108-18, discusses Spenser's political and literary reasons for using Merlin in The Faerie Queene, but does not discuss either the content of his prophecy or

Britomart's change of character type. Michael O'Connell, _Mirror and Veil_ (Chapel Hill: Univ. of North Carolina Press, 1977), pp. 82-83, and Thomas H. Cain, Praise in _The Faerie Queene_ (Lincoln: Univ. of Nebraska Press, 1978), pp. 127-28, both discuss Merlin's prophecy briefly but do not consider its effect on Britomart or her character change.

[5] The most complete treatment of these discrepancies is by Josephine Waters Bennett, _The Evolution of The Faerie Queene_ (Chicago: Chicago Univ. Press, 1942), pp. 145-48. The most recent article is by Joseph Candido, "The Compositional History of Cantos ii and iii in Book III of _The Faerie Queene_," _American Notes and Queries_, 16 (1977), 50-52. Bennett does not discuss the apparent discrepancy between the two stanzas quoted here (ii.6 and iii.53), nor do any of the critics who wrote on this question between her and Candido. Candido considers the discrepancy a sign of Spenser's failure to revise carefully after a major change in plan.

[6] Britomart's behavior in this respect bears comparison with that of Shakespearean heroines disguised as men for the sake of love.

[7] As Glauce points out in ii.41, heroines such as Myrrhe, Biblis, and Pasiphae were right to feel ashamed of loving. Other examples of lovesick heroines who suffer from shame as well as from lovesickness include Scylla, the heroine of the pseudo-Vergilian _Ciris_, who loves her father's and country's enemy, and Dido (_Aeneid_ I and IV), who had sworn to her late husband never to remarry. The scene between Glauce and Britomart is closely modelled on the scene between Scylla and her nurse in _Ciris_, as Merritt Y. Hughes, _Virgil and Spenser_, Univ. of California Publications in English, Vol. 2, No. 3 (Berkeley, Ca.: Univ. of California Press, 1929), pp. 348 ff., points out. Williams, p. 93, observes that Britomart reacts like an Ovidian heroine, that "Glauce draws our attention to the Ovidian context of perversity and pain by sharply denying its relevance," and that Glauce's speeches and actions "set a norm of health and sanity" which exposes the unreality of Britomart's doubts and fears. On the other hand, Richard A. Lanham, "The Literal Britomart," _Modern Language Quarterly_, 28 (1967), understands neither why Britomart ever suffers shame or despair, p. 435: "Her love looks forward to the best of con-clusions, and she is never led to believe otherwise"; nor why Glauce voices a "suspicion" that Britomart's love was lewdly misplaced, p. 436. Yet Britomart does not learn about her love's destined fulfill-ment until Canto iii, and her own self-blame had led to Glauce's temporarily fearing for her.

[8] Williams observes, p. 94, that Britomart's doubts about her vision of Arthegall were understandable, since the mirror in Eliza-bethan symbolism could "reflect false unreal shadows" or be "the mirror of truth, penetrating the false appearance of things." Fletcher, p. 110, n. 67, identifies the mirror as "the emblem of

wisdom" and later, p. 116, n. 69, comments that "It is not clear to
what extent Spenser is here also playing on the idea of art holding
the mirror up to nature." Whatever the exact significance of the
mirror itself, however, it is clear that Britomart's vision resulted
from God's making use of the mirror's magical properties.

[9] Berger, p. 40, notes the shift in emphasis from Merlin's statement that "[God] Guided thy glaunce" in iii.24 to his directive to
"guide the heavenly causes" in iii.25.

[10] Berger, p. 42, comments that "The tree is a resolving image:
it crystallizes the whole historical process in a single figure and
under the double aspect of sexual and natural activity."

[11] Berger, p. 42, disagrees, claiming that the "epic struggle
[is] noted here chiefly for its costliness" and that the stanza moves
"from good to bad," despite the "forcefully imposed" happy ending.

[12] Carrie Anna Harper, The Sources of the British Chronicle History
in Spenser's Faerie Queene (Philadelphia: John C. Winston, 1910), pp.
143-44, notes that Spenser could have found Arthegall's name in the
lists of knights of the Round Table in either Geoffrey of Monmouth's
or John Hardyng's historical chronicles.

[13] Berger, p. 45, comments that most of this section presents
"clear-cut moral issues (good Britons, bad enemies)."

[14] Berger, p. 45, considers Gormond both "bestial and oceanic."

[15] Williams, p. 95, suggests the analogy: God "deals with the
Britons as did Jehovah with the Hebrews, supporting, checking, [and]
punishing." Berger, p. 47, makes two comparisons: "the Britons are
treated like Egyptians in stanza 40 . . . . In the next stanza they
resemble stiff-necked Hebrews whom the Heavens have decreed to displace."

[16] So also Williams, p. 95. Berger, p. 47, disagrees, blaming
the Britons' fall from power on "a failure of racial ethos." O'Connell,
p. 82, argues that "Merlin gives ambivalent reasons for their defeat,"
since the magician speaks both of the "full time prefixt by destiny"
and of "their sinnes dew punishment" (iii.40, 41). I would respond
that Spenser considered "prefixt by destiny" not a "classical and
epic" explanation, as O'Connell sees it, but equivalent to "ordained
by God" and so synonymous with the second line quoted by O'Connell.
Cain, p. 127, reads the prophecy as Williams and I do: history is
"organized behind the scenes by heavenly justice which rewards virtue,
punishes vice, and guides destiny."

[17] Harper, pp. 145-57, discusses the relevant chronicle passages
and their relationship to Spenser's fiction. Her conclusion that
Arthegall's son must be the chronicles' Aurelius Conanus has been
generally accepted. Interestingly, the earliest known annotations to

The Faerie Queene, dated 1597 and written by one John Dixon of Kent, include the following note opposite Spenser's description of Arthegall's son: "Aurelius Conanus the sonne of Artegall and Britomart. rainged [sic] 2: ye: and died." Dixon's annotations have been partially reproduced and analyzed by Graham Hough, The First Commentary on The Faerie Queene (Privately published, 1964); this note occurs on p. 17.

[18] Harper, pp. 159-62. Cain, p. 127, notes that Spenser invented Oswald's bloodless victory to show that God guides human history.

[19] O'Connell, p. 82, observes that "Spenser actually seems to have made more conclusive and final the account of the Britons' end-- almost as if to diminish their glory."

[20] Harper, p. 181, identified the ultimate source of stanza 45 as Caradoc of Llancarfan, whose chronicle of Welsh history has been lost. Rudolf B. Gottfried, "Spenser and The Historie of Cambria," Modern Language Notes, 72 (1957), 9-13, shows that Spenser must have known and used throughout Merlin's prophecy a chronicle called The Historie of Cambria, edited and expanded by David Powell from an English translation by Humfrey Llwyd of Caradoc's work and published in 1584. Gottfried notes, pp. 12-13, that Spenser follows Powell in his description of Howell Dha, but that he confuses Rhodorick the Great with his predecessor Rhodorick Molwynoc and Griffith ap Conan apparently with either Griffith ap Llewellyn or Griffith ap Rhys. Nevertheless, Spenser did not invent his descriptions of Welsh princes' great valor and virtue, but merely assigned the descriptions he found to princes with similar names. Berger, p. 48, says that Merlin's treatment of these three characters "has the effect of praising them for personal qualities and 'nice tries' while relegating them to the back country."

[21] Berger, p. 49, makes the same observation.

[22] Cain, p. 128, notes that "a sparke of fire" in stanza 48 echoes "the old sparkes . . ./ Of native courage" in stanza 45 and so links Henry Tudor to the Welsh princes from whom he descends.

[23] Williams, p. 96, quotes only the first four lines of stanza 49 and observes that they describe "The eventual union of Briton and Saxon under the Welsh and English Elizabeth." Berger, p. 51, claims that stanza 49 moves "downward from perfection to problems: from eternal union to the resolving image of the royal virgin, whose gesture seems purely symbolic and hieratic until the white rod suddenly becomes the emblem of a weapon and a war," but he also, p. 50, comments on the "complex assimilation of racial elements into a political concordia." Fletcher, p. 117, notes that Merlin shows "the political destiny of the kingdom" to involve the union of "Welsh, British, Scotch, and their invader-conquerors, the Saxons

and Normans." Spenser, of course, always used "British" for all of the pre-Saxon peoples. O'Connell, p. 83, likewise observes that "The emphasis is on the Vergilian theme of assimilation of peoples rather than on the more obviously political matter of 'return'." Cain, p. 127, remarks on "the melding in Elizabeth of royal Saxon and rekindled British tradition." Everyone ignores the Danes.

[24] Fletcher, p. 118, observes that "The vision of Merlin is focused on resistance to foreigners without and traitors within."

[25] Cain, p. 127, remarks that Merlin's account "is drastically foreshortened . . . to increase the proximity of the British line and the Tudors."

[26] Berger, p. 51, assumes that Merlin does see an "unrevealed ghastly spectacle" and suggests that it consists of "the international events detailed in Book V." These are, however, quite clearly alluded to in the last lines of the previous stanza. James Nohrnberg, The Analogy of The Faerie Queene (Princeton: Princeton Univ. Press, 1976), p. 633, also assumes the worst: "Merlin baulks at a further prevision of a catastrophic development." Cain, p. 128, recognizes the validity of both positive and negative readings: "This is encomiastic outdoing: the future without the queen cannot be contemplated. But it also articulates the ominous problem of the succession and retrospectively overcasts the whole prophecy."

[27] Britomart reveals her familiarity with Britain's early history and her own family tree in Canto ix of Book III, in a conversation with Paridell about their Trojan ancestry. Spenser's reader has good reason to recognize Bunduca, Guendolene, and Martia, three of Glauce's four examples, from their appearance in the chronicle of British history which Arthur reads in II.x.

[28] Roche, p. 61, argues for interpreting Britomart as an image of discordia concors, citing the Saxon armor as one piece of evidence. Williams, p. 96, speaks of "a union of powers in Britomart herself. . . . She is strong because she is loving and loving because she is strong." O'Connell, pp. 83-84, considers several of the ways in which Britomart and Elizabeth are both symbols of discordia concors, although he limits his discussion to the union of the races which Britomart foreshadows and the queen fulfills, and does not refer to the Tudor emphasis on their uniting the rival branches of the royal house after the civil wars. Cain, p. 127, covers the same points as O'Connell, but more briefly. It might be argued, though it seems not to have been, that the marriage of Britomart and Arthegall itself represents the union of two former enemies, because Britomart, as Merlin reminds her and us, is the descendant of Trojan nobility and Arthegall, according to her vision of him in Merlin's mirror, wears the armor of the Greek Achilles.

Chapter 3

THE SITE OF ROME AND THE SHIELD OF AENEAS

Aeneid VIII opens with Turnus gathering allies to make war on the

Trojans camped in Latium. Vergil uses a remarkable simile to depict

Aeneas' anxiety about the situation:[1]

> Seeing all these things, the Trojan
> hero wavers on a great sea of troubles, and divides his
> swift thought, now here, now there, and rushes in diverse
> directions, and turns over everything, as when the light
> from the sun or from the image of the radiant moon,
> reflected, trembling, by water in bronze bowls, flies
> about everywhere, from side to side.

> quae Laomedontius heros
> cuncta videns magno curarum fluctuat aestu,
> atque animum nunc huc celerem nunc dividit illuc
> in partisque rapit varias perque omnia versat,
> sicut aquae tremulum labris ubi lumen aënis
> sole repercussum aut radiantis imagine lunae
> omnia pervolitat late loca,

(8.18-24)

The events of Book VIII allay Aeneas' anxieties in two ways. He pre-

pares for battle physically by acquiring allies of his own and by

receiving weapons and armor from his mother, Venus. He also prepares

emotionally for combat, by moving into a more personal involvement

with the land for which he fights and by clarifying his understanding

of the ambivalent relationship between violence and civilization.

Excluding journeys, the human action of Book VIII occurs in three

places: the Trojans' camp near the mouth of the Tiber; a settlement of

Arcadians on the site of Rome, called Pallanteum; and the valley where

75

Venus meets Aeneas to give him his arms. The action begins with a dream Aeneas has, in which Tiberinus, god of the Tiber, appears to him. The god advises him to travel up the river to Pallanteum to seek the support of its founder, Evander. Upon doing so, Aeneas receives both the Arcadians' support and that of the Etruscans, who have delayed attacking Turnus until they could find the foreign general that their soothsayer required. When the Trojans pause for rest on their journey from Pallanteum to the Etruscans' camp, Venus brings Aeneas the arms Vulcan has made for him. Aeneas now has sufficient troops to win a war and the personal equipment in which to wage one. Each of the places he has gone has contributed to his physical preparations for combat.

Yet much of the action in Book VIII provides no practical assistance. Tiberinus devotes less than a third of his speech to giving Aeneas the information he needs in order to find the Arcadians. Evander does not discuss the Trojans' military needs with Aeneas until the second day of his visit, having spent the first day celebrating a religious festival, explaining its origin, telling Aeneas the history of Latium, and giving him a tour of the settlement. Finally, Vulcan engraves scenes from Roman history on the shield he makes for Aeneas, scenes which magically enhance the shield and which Vergil describes at some length. Although at first glance the river god, the Arcadian king, and the shield's engravings seem to address a wide variety of topics, they all serve one purpose, to show Aeneas how to establish and maintain a civilized way of life despite various threats to it. Thus the events of Book VIII prepare him emotionally and intellectually for the tasks of defeating his opponents and of founding a city for his Trojans.

Tiberinus' speech introduces Book VIII's concern with cities and settlements. He begins by hailing Aeneas as "you who bring back the Trojan city from its enemies to us" (Troianam ex hostibus urbem / qui revehis nobis, 8.36-37), thus recalling the Italian origin of Dardanus, Troy's founder, and he goes on to promise an Italian future for the Aeneadae: "here is a home assured for you" (hic tibi certa domus, 8.39). To show Aeneas his prophetic ability, the river god predicts an omen, the discovery of a white sow nursing thirty white piglets. In Book III, Helenus had predicted the same omen, explaining that it would mark the site of Aeneas' city (3.389-93). Tiberinus adds that Ascanius will name the city he will found in thirty years Alba ("white") to commemorate this omen. When he proceeds to tell Aeneas about the Arcadians, he pays as much attention to the founding and naming of their city as he has paid to the Trojan's future settlements:

> They chose a site and set a city among the mountains:
> Pallanteum, from the name of their ancestor Pallas.
>
> delegere locum et posuere in montibus urbem
> Pallantis proavi de nomine Pallanteum.
>
> (8.53-54)

Evander has already done what Aeneas will soon do; having come from his native land to Italy, he has preserved his heritage by building a new home for his people. The parallels between Evander's accomplishment and Aeneas' task, implicit in Tiberinus' speech, become explicit during the Trojans' visit to Pallanteum.

Shortly after waking from his dream, Aeneas finds the white pigs, thereby proving that he had seen a god. Following Tiberinus' directions, he goes to Pallanteum to seek an alliance with the Arcadians.

There he finds set before him not only Evander's example but that of Hercules, for the Trojans arrive during an annual feast in Hercules' honor and Evander tells them the story of its origin.[2] Some years earlier, a monster named Cacus, a son of the god Vulcan, lived in a cavern under a cliff and preyed on Evander's subjects:

> Here the ground was always steaming with recent bloodshed, and fastened upon the high gates the faces of men were hanging, white with melancholy decay.

> semperque recenti
> caede tepebat humus, foribusque adfixa superbis
> ora virum tristi pendebant pallida tabo.

(8.195-197)

When Hercules pastured his oxen nearby, Cacus stole four bulls and four heifers from the herd. Because of fortifications designed by Vulcan for the entrance to Cacus' cavern, Hercules could not gain entry until he ripped the stone roof off the cave. Then, undeterred by the black smoke Cacus breathed out, Hercules leapt down into his den and strangled him. In honor of the hero, now apotheosized, the Arcadians celebrate the anniversary of their deliverance from the monster.

Hercules, surely, is meant as a model for Aeneas here. Like Hercules, Aeneas must respond violently to violence (that of Turnus and his allies, in Aeneas' case), but only in order to establish peace. Similarities between Cacus and two of Aeneas' opponents strengthen the parallel between Hercules and Aeneas. The flames and smoke which Cacus produces (_ignis_, 8.199; _fumum_, 8.252), and which reveal his original identity as a volcanic deity, recall the smoky fire of the torch with which Allecto kindled Turnus' anger: "She flung a torch at the young man and fixed the firebrand, smoking with gloomy light, beneath his breast" (<u>facem iuveni coniecit et atro / lumine fumantis</u>

<u>fixit sub pectore taedas</u>, 7.456-57). Turnus' most fearful ally,

Mezentius, treats his enemies as savagely as Cacus treated his prey:

> For he would even join dead bodies to living ones,
> matching hand to hand and face to face--such torment!--
> and thus he would kill them with a slow death, in a
> wretched embrace wet with blood and decay.
>
> mortua quin etiam iungebat corpora vivis
> componens manibusque manus atque oribus ora,
> tormenti genus, et sanie taboque fluentis
> complexu in misero longa sic morte necabat.
>
> (8.485-88)

The hymn to Hercules which follows Evander's tale reminds us of

another similarity between Hercules and Aeneas: Hercules' twelve labors

were imposed by "the decrees of adverse Juno" (<u>fatis Iunonis iniquae</u>,

8.292), and Juno has called down upon Aeneas natural, human, and

infernal storms in the course of the <u>Aeneid</u>. Vergil depicts Juno as

the divine manifestation of irrational violence, whose mortal embodi-

ments include Cacus, Turnus, and Mezentius. The story of Hercules'

defeat of Cacus dramatizes the necessity of using force to maintain

a civilized way of life. Aeneas must accept the fact that war is not

only inevitable, but can serve peaceful ends.

While Hercules foreshadows Aeneas' role in the coming war,

Evander represents the good king he must become afterwards. Certainly

their histories offer grounds for comparison. Like Aeneas, Evander

has left his home unwillingly and endured a long sea-journey before

reaching the land assigned by fate, to which his divine mother and

Apollo have guided him (8.333-36). His city delights Aeneas from the

moment the Trojans enter it:

> Aeneas marvels and directs his willing eyes all around;
> he is charmed by the place and gladly both seeks out
> and learns about each of the monuments of earlier men.

> miratur facilisque oculos fert omnia circum
> Aeneas, capiturque locis et singula laetus
> exquiritque auditque virum monimenta priorum.
>
> (8.310-12)

The parallels between Evander's history and that of Aeneas suggest that the Arcadian king sets the Trojan leader an example, and Aeneas' interest in Pallanteum indicates his willingness to profit from that example. The Arcadians have much to teach the Trojans about living simply.[3] Vergil's first description of Pallanteum concludes with the observation that "Evander governed a state without wealth" (res inopes Evandrus habebat, 8.100). The senators have no riches (pauper . . . senatus, 8.105), and the palace is merely "the house of Evander of modest means" (tecta . . . / pauperis Evandri, 8.359-60). Welcoming Aeneas to his home, Evander advises him explicitly to learn from the Arcadians' simplicity:

> "Triumphant Hercules," he said,
> "entered these gates, this king's house received him.
> My guest, dare to despise wealth and make yourself
> also worthy of godhead, and do not be disdainful of
> my limited estate."

> 'haec' inquit 'limina victor
> Alcides subiit, haec illum regia cepit.
> aude, hospes, contemnere opes et te quoque dignum
> finge deo, rebusque veni non asper egenis.'
>
> (8.362-65)

Evander implies that freedom from pride as well as fighting for peace earned Hercules his apotheosis. Thus the city, its founder, and its hero all show Aeneas the right attitude toward riches.

Aeneas needs the Arcadians' contempt for wealth not only as a

ruler but also as a warrior. Throughout the subsequent books of the
Aeneid, those who despoil slain foes of rich goods perish on account
of their greed. Euryalus, "carried away by too much slaughter and
avarice" (nimia caede atque cupidine ferri, 9.354), dies because the
gold helmet he stole betrays his whereabouts and his other spoils
weigh him down. Camilla, seeing a luxuriously armed enemy, "burned
with womanly desire for booty and spoils" (femineo praedae et spoliorum
ardebat amore, 11.782) and tracked her prey so single-mindedly
through the battle that she failed to notice her own pursuer. Aeneas
kills Turnus upon seeing the belt he took from Pallas' corpse upon
his body, a belt which had attracted Turnus by the beauty of its
engravings and the brightness of its gold (10.495-505, 12.940-49).
In contrast, Aeneas tells the dead Lausus, "Keep the arms in which
you rejoiced" (arma, quibus laetatus, habe tua, 10.827), and takes
Mezentius' weapons and armor only as an offering to Mars Ultor
(11.5-11). Freedom from greed and pride promotes Aeneas' victory in
battle as much as it makes Pallanteum attractive in peace.

Evander tells Aeneas about the region's past as well as showing
him its present condition. His tale reveals both the process by
which a ruler establishes civilization and the impulses which threaten
that achievement. Saturn first civilized the native men, a race sprung
from trees, and gave them laws to make them a community. He named
this part of Italy Latium because "he had lain hidden"(latuisset,
8.323) there from the wrath of his son Jove. Moreover, he and Janus
gave their own names to the cities they built on hills adjacent to
Pallanteum: Saturnia, Janiculum. The golden age lasted as long as
Saturn "ruled his people in gentle peace" (placida populos in pace

regebat, 8.325), but "the madness of war and the love of acquisition
came next" (belli rabies et amor successit habendi, 8.327). Then
Ausonians and Sicanians over-ran the land, changing all its place-
names; a cruel giant called Tiber left his name to the river formerly
known as the Albula.[4] Finally, the gods guided Evander to Latium,
where he built the peaceful city of Pallanteum. This account displays
the civilizing activities of law-giving, city-founding, and peace-
keeping, while identifying the impulses which destroy civilization
as violence and greed.

Evander's pastoral community contains no impressive buildings,
but it has many places sacred to some god or spirit. Hercules himself
had built the altar outside the walls at which the Arcadians hold
his festival. One of the city gates and an altar beside it honor
the nymph Carmentis, Evander's mother, who prophesied the greatness
of Aeneas' descendants and of Evander's settlement. A cavern called
the Lupercal, at the western corner of the Palatine, provides the
Arcadians with a site for their worship of Pan Lycaeus.[5] An adjacent
hill and its sacred grove remain unnamed, for the Arcadians do not
know what god haunts that area, inspiring awe and dread, though some
claim to have seen Jupiter sending thunderstorms from the summit.
This tour acquaints Aeneas with the religious rites of Latium and
thereby makes it possible for him to rule Latins as well as Trojans
after his victory.

Indeed, Aeneas' vision of Tiberinus and his visit to Pallanteum
initiate his personal involvement with his new country. Although
his pietas and his father's prophecies had already committed him to

settling in Italy, he discovers this new home for the first time in
Book VIII. Aeneas' eagerness to see and hear all he can indicates
that he considers this discovery exciting. Learning about the
Italian past and present gives the promised future more reality.
Furthermore, as Vergil frequently reminds the reader, Pallanteum
stands on the site of Rome. When the Trojans first sight Pallanteum,
Vergil calls it the city "which now Roman power has raised to heaven"
(quae nunc Romana potentia caelo / aequavit, 8.99-100). He refers to
Evander as "the founder of the Roman citadel" (Romanae conditor arcis,
8.313), and remarks that the Romans still have an altar and a city
gate in honor of Carmentis (8.337-39). Unlike Evander, Vergil can
name the hill haunted by an unknown god: the Capitol, sacred to
Capitoline Jove (8.347-54). Finally, as Evander and his guests
approach his house, "they saw cattle lowing in both the Roman Forum
and the fashionable Carinae" (armenta videbant / Romanoque foro et
lautis mugire Carinis, 8.360-61). These allusions remind the reader
that Pallanteum represents the Roman past, and therefore Aeneas'
visit completes his exposure to the future reality of Rome. In tour-
ing Evander's city, Aeneas walks on the same ground as his descendants
will and views the religious sites where they will worship. Rome
will inherit both Trojan and Latin characteristics. At Pallanteum,
Aeneas becomes acquainted with that part of the Roman heritage which
he had not previously known.

Aeneas' first day in Pallanteum has served three purposes. The
story of Hercules has shown Aeneas that a hero must take violent
action against those who indulge in lawless violence. The Latins

have disobeyed the commands of their own king in attacking the Trojans,
Turnus raged through Book VII (and will rage through Book IX) like
violence personified, and Mezentius has forfeited the obedience of
his subjects by his monstrous cruelty. To win the right to inherit
the realm of peaceful Saturn and pastoral Evander, Aeneas must first
defeat these violent and lawless foes. Moreover, Evander's descriptions
of Saturn, Janus, and Hercules have offered Aeneas models of civilizing
and civilized behavior, and Evander has provided yet another example
himself. Just as the activities of settling, law-giving, and place-
naming are needed to establish a community, so the humility of Hercules
and the simplicity of Evander are needed to maintain one in peace.
These qualities not only show Aeneas how to rule wisely after the war,
but will also help him to achieve his victory. Finally, Aeneas' closer
acquaintance with Latium has made him both willing to fight for the
Trojans' right to settle there and able to rule the Latin people thereafter. Vergil's comments have reminded the reader that Aeneas' visit
to Pallanteum constitutes his first physical contact with Rome. While
literally preparing to defeat and then govern the Latins, Aeneas has
been symbolically preparing to lay the foundations for the Roman way
of life.

In The Faerie Queene, the British chronicle which Arthur reads
serves similar purposes. It teaches the prince that a good ruler must
possess the strength and skill to subdue lawless violence, put down
rebellion, and resist invasion. Furthermore, the chronicle praises
those who settle lands, build cities, name places, and give laws, while
it condemns the proud and greedy characters. Reading the chronicle

prepares Arthur both for the combat he faces immediately and for his eventual task of ruling Britain wisely. Part of its contribution to his future kingship consists of its inspiring him with patriotic devotion, just as part of Aeneas' reaction to Pallanteum consists of increased emotional involvement with his future homeland. Spenser seems to have borrowed not only the themes of _Aeneid_ VIII, but also much of its narrative function, for use in his own work.

In _Aeneid_ VIII, the themes of Aeneas' visit to Pallanteum are treated a second time on the shield which Vulcan makes and Venus delivers to her son. The engravings on the shield depict "Italian deeds and the Romans' triumphs . . . all the lineage of future off-spring from Ascanius and the wars fought in order" (_res Italas Roman-orumque triumphos . . . genus omne futurae / stirpis ab Ascanio pugnataque in ordine bella_, 8.626, 628-29). The scenes which Vergil singles out belong only to the history of Rome, beginning with the infancy of Romulus and Remus:

> And [Vulcan] had made a fertile she-wolf stretched out
> in Mars' green cave; hanging around her teats, twin
> boys played and fearlessly suckled their mother; with
> shapely neck arched, she stroked them in turn and plied
> their bodies with her tongue.

> fecerat et viridi fetam Mavortis in antro
> procubuisse lupam, geminos huic ubera circum
> ludere pendentis pueros et lambere matrem
> impavidos, illam tereti cervice reflexa
> mulcere alternos et corpora fingere lingua.
>   (8.630-34)

Traditionally, the wolf merely fed and guarded the twins until Faustulus, the shepherd who raised them, discovered them. Yet the picture shows them in her den, and Vergil calls her their mother, both of which imply a larger role for her. In addition to nursing the boys, she tries to lick them into shape, as various wild animals supposedly did their young. Her den belongs to Mars, to whom wolves were sacred and who had fathered the twins. Thus the war-god's totemic animal acts as a mother to his sons and tries to form them as she would her cubs. The fierceness of the boys' parentage and early nurture foreshadows the military power and martial spirit of the city they will found.[6]

Near this cave, Vulcan pictured "the Sabine women seized, contrary to custom" (raptas sine more Sabinas, 8.635), on whose account "new war arose between Romulus' men and aged Tatius and his austere Sabines" (novum consurgere bellum / Romulidis Tatioque seni Curibusque severis, 8.637-38). Since the Romans traditionally respected their elders and valued severitas, Vergil favors the Sabine side by noting their king's old age and their sternness of character. Despite the Romans' violent behavior, Romulus and Tatius become allies and rule their united subjects jointly:

> Armed and holding libation cups, they stood before Jove's
> altar and joined in treaties after sacrificing a sow.
>
> armati Iovis ante aram paterasque tenentes
> stabant et caesa iungebant foedera porca.
>
> (8.640-41)

Here a religious rite establishes peace. Jupiter, ruler of gods and men and so the model for all mortal rulers, supervises the civilizing process of unifying the two peoples.[7]

Not far from these Sabine scenes, Vulcan depicted the dismemberment of Mettus Fuffetius in gruesome detail. Mettus, who governed

Alba, had allied himself with Tullus Hostillus, Rome's third king, but deserted him in battle. His subsequent punishment of being torn apart by two four-horse chariots appears on the shield. Vergil emphasizes the justice of Mettus' death with an unsympathetic remark: "But you should have abided by your words, man of Alba!" (at tu dictis, Albane, maneres!, 8.643). The bloodiness of the description serves to reinforce the moral of the story, which is that treachery will be duly punished.

In the next episode, the Romans resist an attempt by the Etruscan Porsenna to reinstate their last king, Tarquin, whom they had exiled for tyrannical behavior. Besieged by Porsenna's army, "the descendants of Aeneas rushed to arms for the sake of freedom" (Aeneadae in ferrum pro libertate ruebant, 8.648), Vergil presents two representatives of this general love of liberty, one male, one female: Horatius defending the bridge until its destruction and Cloelia swimming the river to escape the Etruscan camp. Both illustrate the Republican ideal of service to Rome without regard for personal safety or comfort. Next, Manlius' defense of the Capitol against the Gauls' attack displays the same patriotism. The barbarians' "milk-white necks are bound with gold" (lactea colla / auro innectuntur, 8.660-61), a display of wealth which contrasts sharply with the thatched roof of Romulus' house on the Capitol (8.654). The sacred geese give warning of the approaching Gauls, thereby showing that Rome enjoys the protection of the gods as well as the devotion of her citizens.[8]

Vergil then turns to Vulcan's depiction of the gods' rites:

> Here he had hammered the naked Luperci and the leaping
> Salii with their wool-tufted caps and their shields
> fallen from heaven; chaste matrons led the sacred rites
> through the city in upholstered carriages.

> hic exsultantis Salios nudosque Lupercos
> lanigerosque apices et lapsa ancilia caelo
> extuderat, castae ducebant sacra per urbem
> pilentis matres in mollibus.

(8.663-66)

The Luperci issue forth from the Lupercal, a cavern on the Palatine

which Aeneas saw on his visit to Pallanteum, and the Salii he had

seen celebrating the festival of Hercules there. Therefore these two

sodalities exemplify the continuity of religious worship on the site

of Rome. Furthermore, the connection of the Luperci to wolves and

the dedication of the Roman Salii to Mars make these groups appropriate

to Vergil's description of the shield, which began with the wolf in

Mars' cavern. Finally, the picture of sacred rites observed by matrons

as well as by priests creates an image of a city filled with reverence

for the gods.[9]

Vergil notes next that Vulcan engraved all of Hades on the shield.

He singles out two of the shades in particular:

> And you, Catiline, hanging from
> a jutting cliff and trembling at the Furies' faces;
> and men set apart by piety, to whom Cato gives laws.

> et te, Catilina, minaci
> pendentem scopulo Furiarumque ora trementem,
> secretosque pios, his dantem iura Catonem.

(8.668-70)

Obviously death has not reconciled the old opponents. Catiline, whose

conspiracy threatened the Republic and for whose execution the younger

Cato argued, suffers torments in one part of the Underworld; Cato, who

committed suicide when he saw the Republic doomed, rules the just souls
in another. Fittingly, Vergil's description of scenes from the Republican
period ends with Cato's name.

The engravings which Vergil has described may cause anxiety, depicting as they do Rome repeatedly endangered; but civilization always
wins and peace is always restored. After punishing the Romans with a
war for having seized the Sabine women, the Sabine king allies himself
with Romulus, and they rule a united people jointly. Tullus kills the
Alban traitor, Rome's Republican citizens resist Porsenna's army,
Manlius saves the Capitol from the barbarians, and the Senate orders
the conspirators executed. Thus no instance of lawless violence goes
unchecked, not even the early Romans' violent deception of the Sabines.
Yet the suppression of violence usually necessitates the use of equal
or greater force, as Vergil acknowledges. The maintenance of a civilized
way of life depends on the willingness to use military power when necessary.

A civilized community also exhibits reverence for the gods and
receives protection from them.[10] The Romans honor their gods by celebrating the ancient festivals of the Luperci and the Salii and by
private citizens' participation in religious rites. The gods show their
favor by sending a wolf to rescue the city's founders and sacred geese
to warn Manlius of the Gauls' attack. The final scenes on the shield,
the battle of Actium and Augustus' triumph thereafter, show the Roman
gods protecting their people in war and the honor paid to those gods by
the victorious emperor and the citizens of Rome.

Vergil's description of the battle of Actium, which Vulcan has

placed at the center of the shield, begins with the golden sea, its
white-capped waves, and the bronze fleet. Then he reaches the first
of the commanders:[11]

> Here Caesar Augustus is leading the Italians into battle,
> with the senators and the common people, the household
> gods and the great gods.
>
> hinc Augustus agens Italos in proelia Caesar
> cum patribus populoque, penatibus et magnis dis.
>
> (8.678-79)

Augustus enjoys complete support both on earth and in heaven, from all
the classes of Italian society and from all the deities of Roman
religion. He seems at least a demigod himself, for flames issue from
his temples and the star of his deified father hovers over his head.
His general, Agrippa, appears as a slightly dimmer version of himself,
aided by "favorable winds and gods" (ventis et dis . . . secundis,
8.682) and with the crown he wears, Rome's highest naval award, gleaming on his temples. Against these familiar figures, Vergil sets
"Antony, with barbaric wealth and motley troops" (ope barbarica variis-
que Antonius armis, 8.685), who "brings with him Egypt and the men of
the East and remotest Bactria" (Aegyptum virisque Orientis et ultima
secum / Bactra vehit, 8.687-88). Last comes Cleopatra, whom Vergil
does not yet name but whom he does condemn: "and [Antony's] Egyptian
wife follows, a forbidden thing" (sequiturque (nefas) Aegyptia coniunx,
8.688). As Vergil's comment indicates, the Romans found both Antony's
marriage and Cleopatra's presence at a battle objectionable. Throughout the passage, Vergil's language transforms the war into a clash
of two opposing cultures: one Italian, unified, and blessed by the
gods; the other foreign, diversified, and cursed with shameful leaders.

Describing how the actual combat begins, Vergil exaggerates the size of the ships, claiming they look like floating islands or great mountains sailing on the ocean, so that the battle resembles a catastrophic upheaval. Cleopatra reappears in the midst of the fighting, signalling to her troops with the sistrum, the Egyptian instrument of the great Isis, similar to a tambourine. She has not yet guessed that she will die soon: "nor does she yet look back at the twin snakes behind her" (necdum etiam geminos a tergo respicit anguis, 8.697). After depicting the scene in human terms, Vergil reveals the role of the deities on both sides:

> And monstrous gods of every sort and the barking Anubis
> brandish weapons against Neptune and Venus and against
> Minerva.
>
> omnigenumque deum monstra et latrator Anubis
> contra Neptunum et Venerem contraque Minervam
> tela tenent.
> $\qquad$ (8.698-700)

Just as Rome's anthropomorphic gods accompany Augustus, so Egypt's theriomorphic deities fight on Antony's side. Vergil names only the dog-headed Anubis, and the vagueness of his description increases the monstrosity of these foreign deities. Their conflict with the "great gods" of Rome seems most unequal, like a nameless rabble threatening three characters of well-known might. Then a fourth Roman god enters the contest, and his intervention wins the day:

> Seeing these things, Actian Apollo bent his bow
> overhead; in terror of him, all Egypt and India,
> all Arabia, all the Sabaeans turned their backs.
>
> Actius haec cernens arcum intendebat Apollo
> desuper; omnis eo terrore Aegyptus et Indi,
> omnis Arabs, omnes vertebant terga Sabaei. (8.704-06)

Augustus restored the ancient temple of Apollo at Actium in thanksgiving for the victory, which he, like Vergil, ascribed to the god.

Before leaving the battle, Vergil shows Cleopatra fleeing, "pale
from her death to come" (<u>pallentem morte futura</u>, 8.709). As she sets
sail, Vergil draws our attention to the Nile, mourning for the defeated
and calling them home to his lap, to the safety of his hidden tribu-
taries. Before the fighting began, Vergil called Cleopatra <u>Aegyptia</u>
<u>coniunx</u> and condemned her presence, but in defeat he can afford to
make her pitiful. Likewise, while the combat continued he spoke only
of Egypt's misshapen deities, monstrous to the Roman mind, but afterwards he pictures the Nile caring for his people as Tiberinus does
for the Italian folk. These changes in presentation not only reflect
the generosity victors can afford to show to the vanquished, but also
prepare us for the final scene on the shield, in which the entire known
world becomes Roman territory. Since Egypt enters the Empire as the
emperor's personal province, Vergil's sympathetic treatment of it is
particularly appropriate.

Augustus' homecoming contrasts sharply with Cleopatra's:

> But Caesar, carried within the Roman walls in triple
> triumph, consecrated an immortal offering to the Italian
> gods, three hundred very great shrines all through the city.

> at Caesar, triplici invectus Romana triumpho
> moenia, dis Italis votum immortale sacrabat,
> maxima ter centum totam delubra per urbem.
> (8.714-16)

Vergil calls the shrines a <u>votum</u>, a thank offering or votive offering,
something one promises a god when asking a favor. Augustus must have
made rather generous promises before the victories he celebrates, and

now he keeps his vows. The whole city follows his example of thanking

the gods for their victory:

> There were matrons' choirs and altars in all the temples;
> slain bullocks covered the ground before the altars.
>
> omnibus in templis matrum chorus, omnibus arae;
> ante aras terram caesi stravere iuvenci.
>
> (8.718-19)

Augustus himself sits in front of the temple of Apollo, his patron

deity. As the defeated peoples bring him gifts, he fastens the presents

to the temple doors, thus continually giving Apollo the fruits of his

success. He views a long procession of the conquered races, "as varied

in their languages as in the style of their clothing and weapons" (quam

variae linguis, habitu tam vestis et armis, 8.723). The variety of

peoples in the unified empire is as admirable as the diversity of its

foes at Actium was threatening. Although Augustus' three-fold triumph

celebrates only his victories in Dalmatia, at Actium, and at Alexandria,

Vergil depicts a parade of far-flung peoples, indicative of the universal

extent of Roman authority: two North African tribes, two races of Asia

Minor, two tribes of Scythians from the mouth of the Don and from the

Caspian Sea, and the Morini, "remotest of men" (extremique hominum,

8.727), a tribe of Gauls from the Belgian coast. Rivers also appear

in the procession, representing the peoples who dwell along their

banks: the Euphrates and the Araxes from the eastern boundaries of the

of the empire, and the Rhine from the northernmost edge.[12]

The Roman empire assures peace by creating unity out of the

variety which Vergil pictures in the parade. As the united Italy

which Augustus commanded at Actium replaced the earlier conflicts between Rome and its Sabine, Alban, and Etruscan neighbors, so a unified world will follow the clash of East and West in that battle. The Morini now march peacefully through the streets of the city which other Gauls had once attacked. The wars Rome has fought have served to spread the Roman way of life, a law-abiding, peace-keeping, god-fearing, civilized way of life, among all men.[13]

If Aeneas could understand the engravings on the shield as well as Vergil's contemporaries could, he would see examples analogous to those displayed to him at Pallanteum. Augustus demonstrates the necessity of using force to suppress lawless violence just as Hercules did. Cato, as well as Saturn, shows how to give men laws. Antony's conspicuous consumption and the wealth flaunted by the Gauls, like Evander's example of contentment with a simple style of life, encourage contempt for riches. In Pallanteum, Aeneas saw how to found cities, whereas the shield shows how to establish an empire; but a universal civilization presupposes the foundation of cities and operates on the same principles, though on a larger scale. What we can learn from the shield about man's duties toward the gods and the divine protection given men is very much like what Aeneas saw in the Arcadians' actions and in Evander's history. Therefore, the fact that Aeneas cannot possibly comprehend the shield's full significance need not disturb us. Vergil freely admits his hero's limited understanding of Venus' present:

> He marvels at such things on Vulcan's shield, his mother's gift; not comprehending their significance, he rejoices in the images, lifting to his shoulder his descendants' fame and fates.

> Talia per clipeum Volcani, dona parentis,
> miratur rerumque ignarus imagine gaudet
> attolens umero famamque et fata nepotum.
>
> (8.729-31)

Aeneas' ignorance does not diminish the symbolic value of his action.[14]
At the end of the book which has introduced him to Rome's past, he
shoulders its future, thus becoming the necessary link between the two.
Aeneas must defeat Turnus to bring about the scenes depicted on the
shield, but Vulcan chose those scenes with foreknowledge of Aeneas'
victory. The shield symbolically guarantees his success even as it
literally guarantees his survival.

In The Faerie Queene, the castle of Alma bears some resemblance
to the shield of Aeneas. Each artifact means more to the readers than
it does to the character who views it; just as Aeneas marvels at the
shield without understanding its engravings, so Arthur admires the
castle without suspecting its allegorical significance. Yet the
lessons depicted on the shield and displayed at the castle are not
wholly lost on the characters in either poem, because Aeneas' visit
to Pallanteum and Arthur's reading the British chronicle expose them
to the same truths as the shield and castle would if fully understood.
Furthermore, the symbolic artifact and the explicit example in each
case differ in scale. Vergil first shows Aeneas the attributes which
establish, maintain, and threaten a civilized community such as the
Arcadian settlement, and then shows the readers how those same attributes help or hinder the enlargement of that community. Vergil's
description of the shield's engravings concentrates on two stages of
Rome's development, its unification of the Italian peninsula and its
unification of the known world. The second stage requires the same

virtues and is threatened by the same vices as the first, but both the good qualities and the bad appear in more extreme forms as the physical arena of conflict enlarges. Analogously, Spenser first shows the reader how the soul (Alma) should govern the body (her castle), and then shows Arthur how the ruler should govern his kingdom. Spenser's summary of the chronicle divides into two halves, the first covering primarily internal British affairs and the second covering Britain's increasing interaction with the external world. Here, too, the same qualities determine the course of events in both periods, but they appear more clear-cut as their consequences increase in importance.

One function of Aeneas' shield has no parallel in The Faerie Queene. Venus' gift of weapons and armor allays Aeneas' anxiety about the coming war. He had not sounded confident when he reached Pallanteum, although Tiberinus had told him, "Do not be frightened by the threats of war" (neu belli terrere minis, 8.40). When Pallas asks for their race and purpose, Aeneas identifies his men as Trojans, "refugees whom they [the Latins] have driven away with arrogant war" (quos illi bello profugos egere superbo, 8.118). Sounding somewhat defeatist, he paints Evander a grim picture of what will follow if Turnus wins; his people will oppress all Italy, from the upper sea to the lower (8.146-49). On the next day, he and Achates remain silent after Evander tells them of the Etruscans' need for a commander and of the military aid his Arcadians can offer, and in their silence "they ponder many hard matters in their sad hearts" (multaque dura suo tristi cum corde putabant, 8.522). Yet Evander's speech ought to have set their minds wholly at ease about the outcome of the conflict. Then Venus sends the omen which indicates that she will soon bring Aeneas weapons and

armor for the battle, and immediately Aeneas' mood changes. He

explains the meaning of the omen to the others,[15] adding a defiant

challenge to his enemies:

> My divine mother foretold that she would send this sign,
> if war broke out, and that she would bring arms made by
> Vulcan from heaven for my assistance.
> Alas, what slaughters approach the unhappy Latins!
> What penalties you will pay me, Turnus! How many men's
> shields and helmets and strong bodies you will tumble
> in your waves, father Tiber! Let them ask for battle,
> break their treaties.

> hoc signum cecinit missuram diva creatrix,
> si bellum ingrueret, Volcaniaque arma per auras
> laturam auxilio.
> heu quantae miseris caedes Laurentibus instant!
> quas poenas mihi, Turne, dabis! quam multa sub undas
> scuta virum galeasque et fortia corpora volves,
> Thybri pater! poscant acies et foedera rumpant.
> (8.534-40)

The reminder that the gods favor him inspires Aeneas with confidence.

He remembers the justice of his cause and the fact that fate has

already allotted him the victory.[16]

Thus the shield, together with the other weapons and armor, com-

pletes Aeneas' emotional as well as physical preparations for war. The

arms tangibly represent his divinely appointed mission and thereby

assure him of success. All the events in Book VIII have served to

make Aeneas ready for battle. His vision of Tiberinus and his visit

to Pallanteum have identified him more personally with the land for

which he must fight. The tale of Hercules has shown him that the

suppression of violence, however violently accomplished, wins honor

and deserves reward. In the history of Latium, the example of Evander,

and the nature of the Arcadian settlement, he has seen the attributes of a civilized way of life: simplicity, reverence, and the keeping of the law and of the peace. For the reader, the shield extends these lessons both temporally and geographically by depicting selected scenes from Roman history, while its existence assures Aeneas that he will have a chance to establish such a way of life in Italy for his followers. When Aeneas shoulders the shield, he becomes a champion of civilization, unalterably opposed to the covetous, treacherous, and aggressive qualities of his foes.

Notes

[1] A detailed comparison of Vergil's simile with its sources is found in W. R. Johnson, Darkness Visible (Berkeley: Univ. of California Press, 1976), pp. 84-87. Brief discussions of the simile appear in Viktor Pöschl, The Art of Vergil, trans. Gerda Seligson (Ann Arbor: Univ. of Michigan Press, 1962, rpt. 1970), pp. 146-47; and in J. William Hunt, Forms of Glory (Cardonbale: Southern Illinois Univ. Press, 1973), pp. 53-55.

[2] My discussion of the tale of Hercules and Cacus owes much to three critics. P. McGushin, "Virgil and the Spirit of Endurance," American Journal of Philology 85 (1964) 225-53, examines the parallels between Cacus and Mezentius, pp. 238-39. Michael C. J. Putnam, The Poetry of the Aeneid (Cambridge, Mass.: Harvard Univ. Press, 1966), considers the elements in Vergil's description of Cacus which link him to the other embodiments of Furor in the poem and argues for the tale's functioning as a paradigm for Aeneas, pp. 130-34. G. Karl Galinsky, "The Hercules-Cacus Episode in Aeneid VIII," American Journal of Philology 87 (1966) 18-51, discusses the story in very similar terms but pays particular attention to the parallels between Cacus and Turnus, passim. Vergil's statements that Vulcan fathered Cacus, that Cacus lived inside a mountain, and that Cacus breathed fire and smoke upon occasion, all suggest that Cacus was originally a volcanic deity. The story had been told by Livy (I.vii.4-7) rather differently; Livy's Cacus is a thieving shepherd, his Hercules is a comic figure, and Cacus' fellow-shepherds charge Hercules with murder, a charge Evander dismisses. Accounts later than Vergil's occur in Propertius, IV.ix.1-20; Dionysius of Halicarnassus, Roman Antiquities I.xxxix.2ff.; and Ovid, Fasti I.534ff.

[3] Pöschl, pp. 59-60, discusses the need Aeneas has to be cleansed of Asiatic luxury in order to become "a Roman in his heart," which is the major action of Book VIII as Pöschl reads it. Vergil was probably thinking not so much of any luxurious reputation attached to Trojan Aeneas as of the corruption of wealth that beset Rome after Punic War II. Evander is advising Aeneas to live in the austere fashion of the early Republic, to which simple style of life Augustus attempted to restore Rome.

[4] Presumably the Tiber is named after a cruel giant on account of its annual flooding.

[5] Pan Lycaeus, which is to say Pan as worshipped on Mount Lycaeon in Arcadia (Evander's native country), is taken here to be connected to wolves, as the Greek word for wolf is lykos. The Lupercal was the site of Lupercus' worship, and his name certainly derives from the

Latin word <u>lupus</u>, also "wolf." The identification of the two gods is probably incorrect, and the establishment of the Lupercalia by Evander is certainly not historical, but accounts of the Arcadians' foundation of Lupercus' worship appear in two works later than Vergil's: Plutarch, <u>Quaestiones Romanae</u> 21, and Ovid, <u>Fasti</u> II.271-82.

[6] Putnam compares this first scene to the opening lines of Lucretius' <u>De Rerum Natura</u>, pp. 147-49. He argues that this first scene on the shield is ambivalent, since it is both pastoral and martial, and that it symbolizes both Rome's future strength--continuity of generation-- and its future weakness--recurrent violence. Although I share Putnam's personal disapproval of violence in general and of wars of conquest in particular, I do not believe that Vergil was either a pacifist or an opponent of Rome's acquiring an empire; hence my rather more posi- tive interpretation of this first scene on the shield.

[7] My interpretation of Vergil's description of the early Romans and the Sabines as favoring the latter agrees with C. M. Bowra, <u>From Virgil to Milton</u> (London: Macmillan, 1961), p. 77. Here, and through- out his detailed analysis of the shield's scenes, Bowra closely follows W. Warde Fowler, <u>Aeneas at the Site of Rome</u>, 2nd ed. (Oxford: Basil Blackwell, 1918), p. 104, who describes this scene as "The escape of the Romans of the Palatine from the fruit of their own unscrupulous- ness, by a treaty with the more civilized and moral Sabines." I do not mean, however, to imply that Vergil wholly condemns the Romans' actions towards the Sabine women. The fact that the women stopped the fighting and professed themselves well satisfied with their situation militates against any such extreme statement.

[8] A point also made by both Bowra, p. 77, and Fowler, p. 104.

[9] Some critics have had difficulty seeing any connection between the religious rites and the other events depicted on the shield. Fowler calls the rites "an awkward interruption" and speculates that Vergil described them at Augustus' request, pp. 104, 106. Kenneth Quinn, <u>Virgil's Aeneid</u> (London: Routledge & Kegan Paul, 1968), p. 50, considers the scene "somewhat loosely related to the two stated themes" of Ascanius' descendants and Rome's wars. On the other hand, P. T. Eden, "The Salii on the Shield of Aeneas: Aeneid 8.663-6," <u>Rheinisches Museum</u> 116 (1973) 78-83, connects these lines to the scene immediately preceding and suggests that these religious rites are the city's thanksgiving for the Gauls' defeat. Eden does not point out that his interpretation would set these two scenes exactly parallel to the last two scenes on the shield, the battle of Actium and Augustus' triumph, but that consequence of his suggestion argues in favor of its adoption, since Vergil is adept at parallelism.

[10] In connecting the Romans' <u>pietas</u> to their continued survival and military triumphs, I am developing the reading briefly advanced by Brooks Otis, <u>Virgil</u> (Oxford: Oxford Univ. Press, 1964). Indeed,

throughout my discussion of the shield, I am in complete agreement with Otis, but his summary treatment omits many observations which I make. He sees the main theme of the shield's engravings as "the constant opposition of virtus, consilium and pietas to the forces of violence in Roman history," p. 341, and concludes that, in all the scenes, "violence is defeated, evil is punished, religio observed," p. 342.

[11] Robert B. Lloyd, "Penatibus et Magnis Dis," American Journal of Philology 77 (1956) 38-46, considers the possible source of this phrase in a public inscription and compares its use in Vergil's description of the shield to its use in Aeneid III, in which Aeneas leaves Troy cum sociis natoque penatibus et magnis dis ("with his companions and his son, with the household gods and the great gods," Aen. 3.12).

[12] Pöschl notes that the presence of these rivers near the end of Book VIII recalls the appearance of the Tiber river-god near the beginning of the book, p. 171.

[13] Fowler, paraphrasing T. R. Glover, describes the final scene on the shield as "the triumph of a nation politically, racially, and geographically one, over clan and city," p. 102. Even Putnam, who is reluctant to admit that Vergil could see anything to praise in the Empire, feels that Vergil praises here "that peace gained through might which was the glory of [Augustus'] regime," p. 150. While it is true, as some critics have pointed out, that the defeated peoples bringing their gifts might not have appreciated their conquest as conferring a great benefit upon them, yet one cannot twist Vergil's description of Augustus' triumph into a presentation of their viewpoint.

[14] The only critic whom I have seen argue that Aeneas' ignorance does destroy the shield's value is Johnson: "the beauty of the shield (and the beauty of the poetry) is equivocal, fails finally to enlighten or to redeem Aeneas (or us), however much it may awe him (and charm us)," p. 114.

[15] Putnam, p. 144, claims that Aeneas does not explain the omen to the others. He believes that Aeneas recognizes it as a traditional omen of an impending death, realizes that the death will be that of Pallas, and tactfully refrains from telling Pallas' father, Evander, what he has just learned.

[16] Hunt feels that Aeneas is not wholly ignorant of the shield's significance, but that it is of no use to him anyway: "Even this final climactic revelation on the magic shield does not remove the agony of his choice . . . nor does it offer Aeneas in Italy a basis for confidence or certitude any more substantial than a picture," p. 75.

Chapter 4

THE CASTLE OF ALMA AND THE CHRONICLE OF ARTHUR

In Book II, Canto x of The Faerie Queene, Spenser describes the books being read by two of his characters. Prince Arthur reads Briton moniments, while Sir Guyon, the hero of Book II, reads Antiquitie of Faerie lond.[1] After a four-stanza proem to the canto, Spenser devotes sixty-four stanzas to the British chronicle and seven to the Elvish one. Although the space Spenser gives to this historical material indicates its importance to him, critics have often objected to its presence. They have accused both chronicles, but especially the British one, of being irrelevant to the moral allegory, digressive from the narrative action, and poetically flat.[2] Those who search for historical allegory have paid more attention to Guyon's book, which presents an allegorized account of the Tudors, than to Arthur's, since one cannot look for covert historical allusions in a passage of overt historical narration.[3] Arguing for the poetic necessity of Canto x, Harry Berger, Jr., has shown how the contrast between the histories dramatizes the differences between British and Elvish knights, between Christian and classical values.[4] Yet each character reads only his own book; the significance of the contrast between the books appears to the readers of Spenser's poem, but not to Arthur or Guyon. In this chapter, I shall consider the reason for Arthur's reading the British chronicle, rather than the meaning our reading both accounts yields us. To that

end, I shall first discuss Arthur's actions in the poem in general
and in Book II in particular.

Prince Arthur came to Faeryland in search of Gloriana, the Faerie
Queene, who in a vision had promised him her love (I.ix.13-15). He
does not complete this quest, presumably because Spenser did not
complete the poem.[5] Instead, Arthur spends his time rescuing other
characters and undertaking subsidiary quests. For example, he rescues
the Redcrosse knight from Orgoglio in I.viii, Guyon from Pyrochles
and Cymochles in II.viii, Placidas from Corflambo in IV.viii, Samient
(with Artegall's assistance) from two of the Souldan's knights in
V.viii, and Timias from Disdain in VI.viii. Such rescues result from
chance encounters as Arthur rides along, seeking his beloved. Apparently he needs neither prior knowledge of nor preparation for these
situations. On two occasions, however, the prince volunteers for
larger-scale adventures, and before these he enjoys a rest and receives
instruction. These adventures occur in Books II and V and offer
several grounds for comparison.

In Book II, Arthur and Guyon enter the castle of Alma after
routing the besiegers before her gates (ix.10-17). She gives them a
tour of the castle and lets them read their respective histories
(ix.18-x). Thence Guyon departs on his original quest, which he
completes in Canto xii. As soon as Guyon leaves, the besieging army
renews its attack with unprecedented fury (ix.5-15).[6] Arthur offers
to engage the attackers' captain in single combat and kills him,
thereby ending the siege (xi.16-49). Similarly, in Book V, Arthur
and Artegall reach Mercilla's palace after destroying Malengin, a

robber who preyed upon her subjects (ix.4-19). She entertains them
and bids them witness Duessa's trial (ix.20-50). When two of Belge's
sons come to request aid for her, Arthur asks Mercilla to send him
(x.6-16). He restores Belge to power (x.17-xi.35), while Artegall
completes his own quest (xi.36-xii).

One of the parallels between these two sequences of events links
them to other books also. About three-quarters of the way through
each of Books I, II, IV, V, and VI, Spenser describes a place which
displays the characteristic virtue of the book in a state of perfect
fulfillment.[7] Spenser uses the canto's argument to label each of the
first two places clearly, calling Caelia's home the "house of Holi-
nesse" (I.x) and Alma's castle the "house of Temperance" (II.ix).
Analogously, the Temple of Venus enshrines Friendship (IV.x), the
palace of Mercilla enthrones Mercy, one part of Justice (V.ix), and
the dancers on Mount Acidale embody Courtesy (VI.x). In Books I, II,
V, and VI, the hero's visit to one of these places prepares him to
fulfill his mission in the subsequent cantos of the book. Only in
II and V does Arthur accompany the knight on his visit, and only in II
and V does Arthur volunteer for a mission which he completes in the
following canto of each book. It seems reasonable to assume, then,
that Arthur's visit to the castle of Alma prepares him to accomplish
the task he undertakes during his stay there.

The tour of the castle has three parts.[8] Alma first shows Arthur
and Guyon the building and its staff (II.ix.21-32), then the parlor,
with its ladies and courtiers (ix.33-44), and lastly the turret's
three chambers and their inhabitants (ix.45-60). As Spenser explains

at the beginning of Canto ix, the castle represents "mans body . . ./
Whiles it is kept in sober government" (ix.1). The knights view the
castle wall, made "of thing like to that AEgyptian slime," which "must
turne to earth" (ix.21). Alma takes them back to the front gate (lips),
in order to see the workmanship of the portcullis (nose) and porch
(jaw), adorned with wandering vine and wanton ivy (beard and mustache).
There she introduces them to h er porter (tongue) and his thirty-two
guards in gleaming armor. Within the hall, they meet

> a comely personage,
> That in his hand a white rod menaged,
> He Steward was hight Diet; rype of age,
> And in demeanure sober, and in counsell sage.
> (ix.27)

The marshal of the hall, Appetite, "did bestow / Both guestes and
meate . . . / And knew them how to order without blame" (ix.28).
Evidently Alma considers the proper arrangement of meals important.

Moreover, she does not hesitate to take her guests into the
kitchen from the hall, "ne spard for nicenesse none" (ix.28). There
we find the cauldron of the stomach and the bellows of the lungs. The
chef Concoction, "A carefull man," oversees the cooking, while the
clerk Digestion supervises the servants "in seemely wise" (ix.31).
The kitchen staff wastes nothing usable, but useless matter is "throwne
out privily" through the back door (ix.32). This part of the castle
tour amazes Alma's guests:

> Which goodly order, and great workmans skill
> Whenas those knights beheld, with rare delight,
> And gazing wonder they their minds did fill.
> (ix.33)

As clearly as the kitchen displays the body's digestive processes to
Spenser's readers, it teaches Arthur and Guyon the importance of

proper nourishment. Guyon needs to learn the necessity of eating properly, since he has come to the castle to recuperate after a lengthy faint caused by prolonged fasting. The knight of temperance must refrain from excessive abstinence as well as from excessive indulgence.

The second part of their tour consists of a visit to the parlor, where "A lovely bevy of faire Ladies sate, / Courted of many a jolly Paramoure" (ix.34). When Prince Arthur has chosen a lady to court, he finds her too serious for his taste. He asks why she seems so grave and suggests it ill becomes her, only to receive the following reply:

> Faire Sir, (said she half in disdainefull wise,)
> How is it, that this word in me ye blame,
> And in your selfe do not the same advise?
> Him ill beseemes, anothers fault to name,
> That may unwares be blotted with the same:
> Pensive I yeeld I am, and sad in mind,
> Through great desire of glory and of fame;
> Ne ought I weene are ye therein behind,
> That have twelve moneths sought one, yet no where can her find.
> (ix.38)

Realizing the truth of her retort, Arthur tries to hide his discomfiture, but his change of color betrays him. He turns aside to ask her name and learns that she is "Prays-desire, / That by well doing sought to honour to aspire" (ix.39). Likewise, Guyon chooses a lady whose silence, blushing, and downcast eyes amaze him until Alma explains:

> Why wonder yee
> Faire Sir at that, which ye so much embrace?
> She is the fountaine of your modestee;
> You shamefast are, but Shamefastnesse it selfe is shee.
> (ix.43)

Guyon's response exactly mirrors the damsel's reaction to him; he falls silent, blushes, and averts his gaze. Thus each knight meets his own motivating passion in an unmixed form. The fact that neither knight finds his lady as attractive as he might wish suggests that each one should maintain a balance of qualities rather than let a single drive dominate. Temperance requires one to temper all one's impulses, the good as well as the bad. Alma's explanation of Shame-fastnesse and Prays-desire's self-explanation make this lesson as plain to the knights as to us.[9]

From the parlor of the heart, Alma takes her guests up into the turret of the head. Of its many rooms, Spenser describes only "three of the chiefest, and of greatest powre" (ix.47). These chambers house Alma's counsellors:

> The first of them could things to come foresee:
> The next could of things present best advize;
> The third things past could keepe in memoree.
>   (ix.49)

Arthur and Guyon visit them in the order listed. The first, youthful Phantastes, lives in a room filled with flies, which Spenser identifies as fantasies, dreams, visions, prophecies, fictions, and lies. Alma's second counsellor, an unnamed "man of ripe and perfect age" (ix.54), dwells among paintings of wisdom and knowledge. Finally the knights reach the hindmost room, home of "an old oldman" (ix.55) named Eumnestes. He sits surrounded by books and scrolls, attended by a boy who fetches him whatever he wishes. These counsellors represent the mental faculties of imagination, judgment, and memory.[10]

Since government depends upon the ruler's exercising good judgment, the second room in the turret includes pictures "Of commen wealthes, of states, of pollicy" (ix.53). Not surprisingly, Arthur and Guyon find Judgment so attractive "That his disciples both desir'd to bee"

(ix.54). Alma does not permit them to linger, however, but leads them
immediately to the third chamber. There the knights come across the
historical chronicles of their native lands:

> Whereat they burning both with fervent fire,
> Their countries auncestry to understond,
> Crav'd leave of Alma, and that aged sire,
> To read those bookes; who gladly graunted their desire.
>   (ix.60)

Arthur and Guyon must understand the past before attempting to judge
the present. Just as the complexity of Alma's arrangements for
feeding her guests indicated the importance of proper physical nourishment, so her decision as to which counsellor they should learn from
indicates the necessity for appropriate food for the mind. Moreover,
Alma does not allow the knights to neglect their bodies in order to
satisfy their hunger for knowledge:

> So long they red in those antiquities,
> That how the time was fled, they quite forgate,
> Till gentle Alma seeing it so late,
> Perforce their studies broke, and them besought
> To thinke, how supper did them long awaite.
> So halfe unwilling from their bookes them brought,
> And fairely feasted, as so noble knights she ought.
>   (x.77)

In order to govern themselves as well as Alma governs her castle,
Arthur and Guyon must exercise moderation in all things.

   Throughout the castle tour, Spenser emphasizes the great respect
shown to Alma by her subjects. The guards "did obeysaunce," the
steward and the marshall "Did dewty to their Lady," and the damsels
and courtiers in the parlor "all attonce out of their seates arose, /
And to her homage made" (ix.26, 28, 36). Their behavior towards her
indicates the excellence of her rule over them. Furthermore, as we
have seen, she rules her guests firmly, insisting on their seeing

the kitchen, not permitting them to study under Judgment, encouraging
them to learn from history, and advising them to care for both their
bodies and their minds. To Arthur and Guyon, she appears to be a
perfect castle governor: courteous to her servants and guests, yet
respected and obeyed; advised by the wisest of counsellors, yet clearly
exercising authority over them. To Spenser's readers, she displays
the soul's proper governance of the body. Spenser saw the state, the
household, and the individual as analogous bodies, each a microcosm
of the universe and each ruled by a single head. Alma's excellent
government of her household, therefore, teaches Arthur and Guyon the
same lessons as the allegorical significance of Alma and her castle
teaches us.[11]

The lessons taught at the castle of Alma all concern temperance,
or self-government. Arthur and Guyon have learned to exercise care
in feeding their bodies and their minds properly and to maintain a
healthy balance among their passions and between their physical and
intellectual needs. Moreover, Alma has provided an example of good
government on a larger scale by the wise authority with which she rules
her household and tends her guests. The examples set before Aeneas
in Aeneid VIII also concerned temperance and rulership, although the
emphasis differed. Evander shows Aeneas the threat violence poses to
society, and he warns his guest against being proud of wealth or greedy
for it. Violence and avarice are, of course, forms of intemperance;
therefore, Furor and Mammon test Guyon in Book II of The Faerie Queene.
In addition to depicting the dangers of intemperate behavior, Evander,
like Alma, provides an example of good government. Both rulers instruct

their guests in history, Evander orally and Alma by permitting them
to read the chronicles they find in the chamber of memory. The
British chronicle which Arthur reads not only develops the themes
of intemperance and rulership more fully, but also treats another
topic of Aeneid VIII: the process by which a civilized community is
founded and maintained.

The British chronicle divides into two sections of equal length.[12]
In the first half (x.5-36), Spenser describes the island's prehistori-
cal state, its conquest by Brutus, and his descendants' reigns. This
section ends when Brutus' line dies out. In the second half (x.37-68),
the emphasis shifts from internal to external affairs. Whereas the
chief dangers in the earlier period come from strife between members
of the royal family, in the later period the dangers derive primarily
from invasions of Britain by foreigners. The first section depicts
the pacification, naming, and settlement of land as a good ruler's
activities; the second section adds political unification, law-giving,
and the expression of religious reverence to the list.

Spenser begins his account by observing that ancient Britain,
a "salvage wildernesse, / Unpeopled, unmanurd, unprov'd, unpraysd"
(x.5), did not "deserve a name" (x.6). Then mariners, guiding their
ships by the white cliffs, began to call the island Albion. Unknown
to them, the land did have inhabitants, "hideous Giants, and halfe
beastly men, / That never tasted grace, nor goodnesse felt" (x.7).
Spenser relates the story of Dioclesian's daughters coupling with
fiends to bring forth these giants, but he considers it hard to believe
("uneath to wene," x.8). He inclines rather to their having sprung

from the earth which their way of life disgraced:

> They held this land, and with their filthinesse
> Polluted this same gentle soyle long time:
> That their owne mother loathd their beastlinesse,
> And gan abhorre her broods unkindly crime,
> All were they borne of her owne native slime.
>
> (x.9)

This situation continues until Brutus, "anciently deriv'd / From royall stocke of old Assaracs line," comes to the island and deprives the giants "of their unjust possession" (x.9.). Three of his comrades offer noteworthy assistance, Corineus by slaying Goemot, Debon by trapping Coulin, and Canutus by defeating Godmer. In return, Brutus grants them portions of land which they name after themselves: Cornwall, Devonshyre, and Canutium, now Cantium or Kent, respectively. Brutus subdues the entire island, killing all the race of giants, and calls it Britany.

Thus various regions of Britain, which received its first name only when it became useful to mariners, commemorate the victories of Brutus and his companions over the bestial giants. Tracing place-names to such figures apparently mattered to Spenser enough for him to invent the tales of Debon and Canutus.[13] Moreover, he describes the giants as far more degraded than his sources portray them as being, and insists on their complete elimination rather than their flight from or submission to Brutus' men.[14] Taken together, these changes provide not merely justification for Brutus' conquest, but glorification of it. He and his followers become champions, saving the land from savage oppressors, naming and settling the wilderness.

Spenser sums up Brutus' character as king in one line: "Lov'd

of his friends, and of his foes eschewd" (x.13). He leaves his realm
divided among his sons, with Locrine as overlord, Albanact ruling in
the north, and Camber in the west. Following the previous generation's
example, they name their shares after themselves, so that modern England,
Scotland, and Wales acquire their ancient names of Logris, Albania,
and Cambria. The brothers rule in perfect concord:

> And each his portion peaceably enjoyd,
> Ne was there outward breach, nor grudge in hart,
> That once their quiet government annoyd,
> But each his paines to others profit still employd.
>
> (x.14)

An invasion disturbs their peace, but Locrine routs the invaders.
Attempting to flee the king's pursuing army, the barbarian chieftain,
Humber, drowns in the river Abus, which thereafter assumes his name.
This event provides an interesting parallel to the renaming of the
river Albula, in _Aeneid_ VIII, after a giant called Tiber (_Aen_. 8.330-
32).

Locrine's pride in his triumph leads to his downfall. "Proud of
victorie, / And insolent," the king takes a mistress (x.17).[15] Queen
Guendolene raises an army, captures the lovers, imprisons her husband
for life, slays his mistress, and drowns their illegitimate daughter,
Sabrina. The river in which Sabrina dies becomes the Severne in her
memory. Guendolene proceeds to rule the kingdom temporarily:

> Then for her sonne, which she to Locrin bore,
> Madan was young, unmeet the rule to sway,
> In her owne hand the crowne she kept in store,
> Till ryper years he raught, and stronger stay:
> During which time her powre she did display
> Through all this realme, the glorie of her sex,
> And first taught men a woman to obay:
> But when her sonne to mans estate did wex,
> She surrendred, ne her selfe would lenger vex.
>
> (x.20)

Some critics find Guendolene intemperate, either for her "wrath and cruelty" toward Estrild and Sabrina,[16] or for her "usurpation" of the throne.[17] Spenser seems to agree with the former charge when he calls Sabrina "the sad virgin innocent of all," but he ends his account of her death and her mother's with a moral which puts the blame of Locrine and Estrild: "Such was the end, that to disloyall love did fall" (x.19). Nor does he describe the queen as ambitious. Guendolene does not wear the crown, but keeps it in trust for her son, and she finds ruler-ship more vexatious than desirable. Spenser stresses the king's intem-perance, his "vaine voluptuous disease" (x.17), more than any error on the queen's part.[18]

Spenser covers the next two reigns as quickly as possible. Madan proves "unworthie of his race: / For with all shame that sacred throne he fild" (x.21). He leaves the crown jointly to his two sons, but Memprise kills Manild "For thirst of single kingdome" (x.21). Although several chronicles relate that wild animals devoured Memprise after he had ruled tyrannically for twenty years,[19] Spenser omits any account of his reign and of his death, passing instead directly from the act of fratricide to Memprise's admirable successor, Ebranck.

Ebranck restores the family's reputation by his continental triumphs, but he finally retreats from France in defeat. Meanwhile, his twenty sons, "which did apply, / Their minds to praise, and chevalrous desire," conquer Germany, which takes its name from "Those germans" (siblings), just as the regions of Britain took their conquerors' names (x.22).[20] The restoration of past glory becomes more evident with Ebranck's heir, "The second Brute, the second both in name, / And

eke in semblance of his puissance great" (x.23). He avenges his
father by his conquest of France, a "recompence of everlasting fame"
(x.23).[21] As a result of his deeds, his son Leill "Enjoyd an heritage
of lasting peace" and built two cities, Cairleill and Cairleon (x.25).
Huddibras, Leill's successor, reigns peacefully after him. Then
Bladud, having studied in Athens, brings philosophers back "to these
salvage parts, / And with sweet science mollifide their stubborne
harts" (x.25). The city-building, peace-keeping, and educating activities of these three kings represent not merely a recovery of but
an advance beyond the state of civilization attained by the first
Brutus. Indeed, the hot baths Bladud constructs at Bath aid other
countries' citizens as well as his own subjects, for "to their people
wealth they forth do well, / And health to every forreine nation"
(x.26). Yet a man should not place too much trust in his skill, as
Bladud's example shows; he falls to his death when overconfidence
leads him to attempt flight.[22] On the whole, however, the kings following Brute II improve upon his achievements as markedly as those
following Brute I declined from his standard of excellence.

Spenser next devotes six stanzas to the story of Leyr (x.27-32).
Intending to divide his realm among his three daughters, he asks
which one loves him most. Cordelia's "simple answere," that "she
lov'd him, as behoov'd," angers him into disinheriting her (x.28).
Leyr then abdicates in favor of Gonorill and Rigan, whose hospitality
afterwards fails to match their protestations of love. When he visits
Cordelia, she welcomes him, makes war upon her sisters, and restores

him to the throne. Leyr has made three mistakes, in judging his
daughters by words rather than deeds, in relinquishing the kingship,
and in dividing the kingdom. Once he realizes the first error, Cordelia
rights the second and third. Having learned from his experience, Leyr
leaves the entire realm to her when he dies. She "peaceably the same
long time did weld: / And all mens harts in dew obedience held"
(x.32). Yet one cannot so easily rectify a king's errors in judgment.
Two of Cordelia's nephews, remembering their mother's brief rule,
rebel against the rightful queen. Seizing the crown, they imprison
Cordelia for so long that she hangs herself, "wearie of that wretched
life" (x.32).[23]

Cundah and Morgan, the usurping brothers, repeat the mistake
Memprise and Manild made and try to rule jointly. Cundah finds it
intolerable "To have a pere in part of soveraintie," starts and wins
a civil war, and kills his brother in a part of Wales later called
Glamorgan (Morgan's land) on his account (x.33). Cundah bequeathes
Britain to his son Rivallo, "In whose sad time bloud did from heaven
raine" (x.34), a fact which does not dispose the reader to think well
of the monarch, about whome Spenser says nothing else. Two monarchs
following Rivallo rule "In constant peace" and two succeeding monarchs
rule without any qualifying comment whatsoever (x.34).

Having rushed through five generations in as many lines, Spenser
reaches the reign of Gorbogud, whose "ambitious sonnes" imprison him
in order to take his place (x.34). Predictably, "the greedy thirst
of royall crowne, / That knowes no kinred, nor regardes no right,"
causes Porrex to depose his brother Ferrex from the shared kingship

(x.35). Ferrex invades the country with a foreign army to regain his position but dies in battle. To avenge his death, his mother kills her other son, Porrex, while he sleeps. Spenser completely disapproves of her action, calling her "his mother merciless, / Most mercilesse of women," and saying that she "with most cruell hand him murdred pittilesse" (x.35). Her unnatural deed marks the lowest point reached in the history of Brutus' descendants, and it brings their line to an end.

Spenser's lament for the end of this dynasty reminds the reader that good rulers as well as bad had sprung from Brutus:

> Here ended Brutus sacred progenie,
>   Which had seven hundred yeares this scepter borne,
>   With high renowme, and great felicitie;
>   The noble braunch from th'antique stocke was torne
>   Through discord, and the royall throne forlorne:
>   Thenceforth this Realme was into factions rent,
>   Whilest each of Brutus boasted to be borne,
>   That in the end was left no moniment
> Of Brutus, nor of Britons glory auncient.
>
>   (x.36)

Berger feels that "these formulae of praise are almost ironical," but he also reads the first half of the chronicle as a record of "almost uninterrupted mayhem."[24] Yet Spenser has devoted as much space to positive exempla as to negative.[25] Brutus and many of his successors earned their "high renowme" by killing evil giants, naming and settling lands, and building cities and medicinal baths. Still, strife has repeatedly torn the royal family. Civil war broke out between Locrine and Guendolene, Cordelia and her sisters, Cundah and Morgan, Ferrex and Porrex; Memprise, Cundah, and Porrex committed fratricide; Cordelia's nephews imprisoned her, as Gorbogud's sons did him; and the most unnatural act, a mother's slaying of her own son, caused Brutus' line to die out. With the exceptions of Locrine's punishment and Gorbogud's deposition, all the occasions of strife derive from attempts to divide the kingdom or to share the kingship. The ideal government, exemplified by Brutus and his comrades and by Locrine and his brothers before his adultery, consists of a single strong central authority, supported by lesser rulers in the farther reaches of the realm. When Porrex' murder ends the line of Brutus' descendants, complete anarchy results, as the second half of the stanza quoted above indicates. In slaying the last heir to the throne, Porrex' mother acted without pity for the country as well as without mercy for her son.

In the first half of the chronicle, Spenser consistently praises those figures--Brutus, Corineus, Debon, Canutus, Locrine, Ebranck, and Brute II--who use their personal strength and military ability to subdue lawless violence, resist invasion, or enlarge the British kingdom by foreign conquest. The defeat of the giants by Brutus and his companions recalls the story of Hercules and Cacus in Aeneid VIII, and Spenser's admiration for militarily successful British rulers echoes Vergil's praise of the Roman leaders depicted on the shield of Aeneas. Throughout this period of British history, good kings and captains leave their names to the lands they settle and the cities they found, whence derive the names Britain, Cornwall, Devenshire, Kent, Logris, Albania, Cambria, Germany, and Cairleill. On the other hand, rivers commemorate the barbarian Humber and illegitimate Sabrina, and

part of Wales preserves the memory of Morgan's murder by his brother.
As Aeneas learns at Pallanteum, ancient Italian place-names serve
analogous functions; the names of two cities, Janiculum and Saturnia,
honor their founders (Aen. 8.357-58), but Latium recalls Jove's perse-
cution of his father (Aen. 8.319-23), the Tiber river commemorates a
cruel giant (Aen. 8.330-32), and Ausonian and Sicanian invaders changed
the names of many places (Aen. 8.328-29). Vergil and Spenser agree
both that naming a place is part of the process of civilizing it and
that acts of violence often cause place-names to be changed. The
names of cities, rivers, and regions thus form a record of good men's
attempts to establish a civilized way of life and of bad men's attacks
on civilization.[26] Finally, the first half of the British chronicle
reveals that the pride exhibited by Locrine and the ambition shown by
Memprise, Cundah, Morgan, Porrex, and Ferrex are the qualities which
threaten the kingdom. Just as Evander warns Aeneas against arrogance
and greed for wealth (Aen. 8.362-65), so the book which Arthur reads
warns him against arrogance and greed for power. All of the lessons
taught in the first half of the chronicle will be reinforced in the
second half, but new developments in British history will teach Arthur
some new lessons, also.

The second half of the chronicle begins, as the first half
began, with the pacification of the island by a new king, whose activities and attributes serve as the model for subsequent generations.
Donwallo represents an advance on Brutus in many respects. He shows
himself free from ambition by the way in which he comes to the kingship:

> Then up arose a man of matchlesse might,
>   And wondrous wit to menage high affaires,
>   Who stird with pitty of the stressed plight
>   Of this sad Realme, cut into sundry shaires
>   By such, as claymd themselves Brutes rightfull haires,
>   Gathered the Princes of the people loose,
>   To taken counsell of their common cares;
>   Who with his wisedom won, him streight did choose,
> Their king, and swore him fealty to win or loose.
>   (x.37)

Although the savagery of the giants justified Brutus' conquest of their

land, he remained a self-elected king. The British nobles select

Donwallo as their ruler, thus giving him as much authority as Brutus

had, and they base their choice on his fitness to rule, on his wisdom

and his compassion for the people, qualities which transcend those

displayed by Brutus or any of his descendants. This selection, which

has absolutely no foundation in any of the historical chronicles,[27]

does not so much restore the monarchy as start a new form of govern-

ment, one in which the king acts in the best interests of those he

governs.

Donwallo proceeds to unify the country by defeating those who

had claimed various portions of it. Spenser emphasizes the upstart

character of these claimants, one "of Logris miscreate," another

"of Albanie newly nominate," a third "of Cambry king confirmed late"

(x.38); none of Donwallo's rivals has a better right to the throne

than his. The king creates a "quiet state" and gives the people

"civill governaunce" throughout the newly united realm (x.38). Having

established peace nationally, Donwallo makes laws to maintain justice

and prohibit violence individually:

> Then made he sacred lawes, which some men say
>   Were unto him reveald in vision,
>   By which he freed the Traveilers high way,
>   The Churches part, and Ploughmans portion,
>   Restraining stealth, and strong extortion;
>   The gracious Numa of great Britanie:
>   For till his dayes, the chiefe dominion
>   By strength was wielded without pollicie;
> Therefore he first wore crowne of gold for dignitie.
>   (x.39)

Spenser has made no previous mention of any religious observance on any king's part, but the sacredness of Donwallo's laws, their possibly divine revelation to him, and their protection of the Church's rights all indicate Donwallo's religious reverence. Spenser's comparison of Donwallo to the Roman Numa is crucial. Numa's role as the first law-giver of ancient Rome provides the obvious point of comparison, and Spenser's audience would have known other important parallels. For instance, Numa, like Donwallo, was selected by the elders (after Romulus had died without an heir), and Numa, too, had a matchless reputation for piety and wisdom. Perhaps we should also cite the fact that when Numa succeeded Romulus, it was as a man of peace and law succeeding a man of strength and action; but without Romulus, Numa would have had no Rome to rule. Similarly, Donwallo's virtues exceeded Brutus' "Strength . . . without pollicie," yet the work of Donwallo in founding a new way of life for Britain rested on Brutus' accomplishment of founding Britain itself. Still, Spenser's closing observation (x.39) stresses the newness of Donwallo's monarchy, the first with enough dignity to wear a golden crown.[28]

His sons Brennus and Bellinus share the throne but spend their energies sacking Rome, ransacking Greece, and subjecting France and

Germany, instead of fighting each other for domestic supremacy (x.40).
Spenser's omission of the traditional wars between the brothers,[29]
like his invention of Donwallo's election, serves to underscore the
difference between this era and the one just past. Bellinus' son
Gurgunt continues the good work of foreign conquest by subduing
Easterland and Denmark. He also manages to gain land and show compassion simultaneously, by settling fugitives from Spain in Ireland
in return for their allegiance to Britain (x.41). In the following
generation, Donwallo's justice and law-giving live again in Gurgunt's
heir, Guitheline, "the justest man and trewest in his dayes," and
in his wife Mertia,

> A woman worthy of immortall prayse,
> Which for this Realme found many goodly layes,
> And wholesome Statutes to her husband brought;
> Her many deemd to have beene of the Fayes,
> As was Aegerie that Numa tought;
> Those yet of her be Mertian lawes both nam'd & thought.
> (x.42)

The comparison of Mertia to Numa's teacher Aegerie serves to suggest
that Mertia's laws equal or even excel those of Donwallo, Numa's
counterpart. Moreover, Mertia gives her name to a legal code, an
instrument of civilization, rather than to a tract of land, the object
of man's civilizing efforts, as characters in the first era did.[30]

Spenser merely lists the next three kings, but he relates the
mixture of good and ill in the fourth, Morindus:

> Who, had he not with wrath outrageous,
> And cruell rancour dim'd his valorous
> And mightie deeds, should matched have the best:
> As well in that same field victorious
> Against the forreine Morands he exprest;
> Yet lives his memorie, though carcas sleepe in rest.
> (x.43)

With Morindus, Donwallo's successors decline from his standard of excellence for the first time, and Morindus' five sons present as complex a mixture of qualities as he had presented. Gorboman leads a "vertuous life," but his brother Archigald, who succeeds him, is deposed "for his proud disdaine" and the throne given to the third brother, Elidure. Spenser does not say who does the deposing and selecting of these monarchs, but whoever it was certainly failed to consult Elidure. Out of pity, Elidure restores Archigald to power and accepts the crown only when the latter dies. Then the fourth and fifth brothers, Peridure and Vigent, imprison Elidure and take his place. He outlives them, however, to rule "long with honorable state," until his own death (x.45). This tangled succession recalls the familial strife of the first era, but with several differences. No one kills anyone else, not even when Peridure and Vigent share the kingship, a situation which always led to fratricide in the earlier period. Elidure survives his imprisonment, unlike those monarchs confined, whether justly or not, in former times. Elidure's restoration contrasts most sharply with Cordelia's despairing suicide in exactly analogous circumstances. Finally, Elidure's willingness to give the crown back to Archigald indicates not merely his freedom from personal ambition but a respect for legal procedure which honors the monarchy despite the monarch's own dishonor.

Spenser summarizes the next thirty-three kings by simply enumerating them: "Even thrise eleven descents the crowne retaynd" (x.45). The last of these, Hely, leaves the kingdom to his son Lud, who in turn

> Left of his life most famous memory,
> And endlesse moniments of his great good:
> The ruin'd wals he did reaedifye
> Of Troynovant, gainst force of enimy,
> And built that gate, which of his name is hight,
> By which he lyes entombed solemnly.
>
> (x.46)

The positive qualities which first appeared in Donwallo did not replace those shown by earlier kings, but supplemented them.[31] Lud deserves as much honor for his building projects, though partly based on previous generations' works, as Leill or Bladud deserved.

Lud leaves two sons too young to rule, Androgeus and Tenantius, wherefore their uncle Cassibalane "Was by the people chosen in their sted" (x.47). During his reign, Julius Caesar invades Britain. Throughout four hundred years of warfare with Rome (x.62), the Britons only lose when betrayed by one of their own. They repel Caesar's first two landing parties, but Androgeus, "envious of Uncles soveraintie," aids the Romans' third attempt (x.48). Tenantius later inherits the realm and keeps the peace. Upon the refusal of his successor, Kimbeline, to pay tribute, war breaks out again. The king dies in battle, "by a Treachetour / Disguised slaine," yet the leadership of his brother Arvirage wins the day despite the traitor (x.51). Marius, Coyll, and Lucius reign after Arvirage without conflict with Rome, but Lucius dies without leaving an heir.

> Whereof great trouble in the kingdome grew,
> That did her selfe in sundry parts divide,
> And with her powre her owne selfe overthrew,
> Whilest Romanes dayly did the weake subdew.
>
> (x.54)

The anarchy resulting from the interregnum constitutes another form

of self-betrayal, one which aids the Roman cause as surely as more
deliberate treason would.

A woman warrior, Bunduca, emerges to lead the Britons. She
triumphs for a time, losing only when "the Captaines on her side, /
Corrupted by Paulinus, from her swerv'd" (x.55). Although she rallies
the survivors and renews the attack, she has lost all hope of another
victory and commits suicide when faced with final defeat. Spenser
describes this act approvingly, as choosing death before dishonor
("Rather then fly, or be captiv'd her selfe she slew," x.55) and as
disappointing her foes ("She triumphed on death, in enemies despight,"
x.56).[32]

The next leader, Fulgent, routs the Roman army, "Yet in the
chace was slaine of them, that fled: / So made them victours, whom he
did subdew" (x.57), and thus becomes another example of self-defeat.
Thereafter rival claimants for the throne battle each other for a
while. Allectus "treacherously" slays Carausius, who had used power
delegated him by the Romans against them (x.57). In turn, Asclepiodate
kills Allectus in battle but falls to Coyll in later combat. When
Coyll, "after long debate," becomes the "first crownd Soveraine"
since Lucius, "Then gan this Realme renewe her passed prime" (x.58).
As a sign of Britain's return to former grandeur, Coyll founds a new
city: "He of his name Coylchester built of stone and lime" (x.58).
Moreover, he marries his daughter Helena to the Roman Constantius,
and their son Constantine becomes emperor of Rome. An earlier inter-
marriage, between Arvirage and the emperor's daughter Genuissa, served

merely to keep peace between the peoples during her lifetime (x.52),

but this union promises a complete unification.

Rome and Britain do not unite, however, because Constantine's

absence on the Continent permits the British Octavius to seize power,

"by unrighteous doome" (x.60). Yet Spenser feels that Octavius'

steadfast enmity to Rome excuses his usurpation:

> But he his title justifide by might,
> Slaying Traherne, and having overcome
> The Romane legion in dreadfull fight:
> So settled he his kingdome, and confirmd his right.
>   (x.60)

History repeats itself when Octavius, having no son, weds his daughter

to the Roman Maximian, who uses the British kingdom he subsequently

inherits to make himself the new emperor. Since Maximian "led away"

(x.62) the British warriors, his assassination leaves the country

without either a ruler or any means of self-defense. Therefore, when

Huns and Picts invade Britain, the people "Were to those Pagans made

an open pray, / And dayly spectacle of sad decay" (x.62). Evidently

one man cannot be king of Britain and emperor of Rome except at the

Britons' expense. Spenser's approval of Octavius' usurpation suggests

his disapproval of such a union, and the disasters which follow on

Maximian's removal of the "war-hable youth" (x.62) prove the folly of

attempting to unite the two.

Spenser never admits that Britain became a province of the Roman

Empire, a fact well-known by his time. Instead he depicts the Britons,

"Whom Romane warres, which now foure hundred yeares, / And more had

wasted, could no whit dismay" (x.62), as militarily superior to the

legions of Rome. The British often defeat themselves, by treason or
by internal dissension, but no external foe can defeat them until
they strip themselves of their warriors in order to acquire the Empire
for their king. No good comes of the ambitions of Constantine and
Maximian in Spenser's account. He omits the finding of the True Cross
by Constantine's British mother Helena and the emperor's own conversion
to Christianity, both of which would imply that Constantine's leaving
Britain for Rome served noble purposes. After altering the traditional
portrait of Constantine by this omission, Spenser merely reported the
story of Maximian as he found it related by others, for the traditional
accounts agreed that Maximian's elevation to emperor resulted in
affliction for the people he should have ruled.[33]

The interregnum begun by Maximian's death continues until the
Britons choose a new king, "Till by consent of Commons and of Peares, /
They crownd the second Constantine with joyous teares" (x.62). This
Constantine rids the land of Huns and Picts and begins to rule in
peace. The "neighbour Scots, and forrein Scatterlings" continue to
annoy the Britons with border raids, however, so Constantine builds
a wall across the island to keep them out (x.63). The historical
chronicles all agree that the Romans built this wall,[34] but Spenser
wishes a British king rather than a Roman emperor to appear concerned
for the safety and comfort of the British people.

Unfortunately, Constantine II dies while his sons are under age,
and their uncle Vortigere usurps the kingship. The princes' tutors
smuggle them into Armorica out of fear of Vortigere, who imports

Saxons to defend him both from the Picts and from the princes. The
Saxon captains, Hengist and Horsus, "making vantage of their civill
jarre," gather enough power to depose Vortigere and reign in his
place (x.65). Vortigere thus becomes another example of self-defeating
ambition and of the dangers of internal dissension in the presence of
foreign troops. Although his son Vortimere restores Vortigere to
power, the king has learned nothing from his experience and pardons
Hengist, "seeming sad, for that was donne" (x.66). Soon afterwards,
the Saxon slays three hundred British lords at a banquet. At this
low ebb of Britain's fortunes, Constantine's sons return and kill
both Vortigere and Hengist to reclaim the crown. Ambrose Aurelius
then "peaceably did rayne," until poisoned by a vengeful Saxon (x.67).
With the words, "After him Uther, which Pendragon hight, / **Succeding**,"
the chronicle comes to an abrupt end, no mark of punctuation even
following the last word on the page (x.68).

In the second half of the chronicle, the positive qualities of
Brutus' line remain admirable. Spenser praises Brennus, Bellinus,
Gurgunt, Morindus, Arvirage, Bunduca, and Octavius for their military
prowess, and Lud and Coyll for the building projects named after them.
Yet Donwallo does inaugurate a new age and sets the standards by which
Spenser judges subsequent monarchs. Donwallo is the first king who
reveres the gods and is favored by them. He is not greedy for power,
and Spenser condemns those who are, whether their ambition leads them
to usurp the British throne or to become the Roman emperor.[35] In the
case of "ambitious Rome" (x.49) itself, Spenser deplores the "hideous

hunger of dominion" (x.47) which prompted Caesar's invasion of Britain.
In contrast, he approves of those, like Bunduca and Octavius, who seek
power only in order to serve their fellow-Britons by defeating the
Romans. Donwallo's promulgation of a legal code and his selection by
the peers of the realm indicate this era's concern with due process,
later exemplified by Mertia's laws, Elidure's refusal to take the
crown from his brother, and the elections of Coyll and Constantine II.
Finally, Donwallo's unification of Britain provides the ideal which
the Britons sometimes struggle to restore by uniting against the Roman
forces but sometimes betray by treacherous behavior or self-defeating
overreaching. The glorious reigns of Coyll and Constantine II result
from their restoration of national unity and renewal of Britain's
defenses against its foes, in marked contrast with the disastrous
consequences of the anarchic interregna preceding their elections.

Thus the second half of the chronicle both reinforces the lessons
of the first half and adds to their number. It remains important that
a leader be strong enough to win foreign wars or to defeat invaders.
Intemperate ambition, whether on the part of Britain's rulers or on
the part of its enemies, continues to pose the most serious threat to
the kingdom. The activities of a good king still include city-founding
and place-naming. In the second era, however, the list of admirable
qualities expands to include respect for the law and reverence for
the gods. The addition of these qualities makes the parallels between
Vergil's and Spenser's depictions of rulership more complete, since
Aeneas finds Saturn's law-giving and Evander's piety set before him

at Pallanteum as good examples, and Cato and Augustus display the same qualities on his shield.

Moreover, the relationship of the two halves of the chronicle to one another resembles the relationship between the shield's earlier and later scenes. In the first era of Roman history, Rome's enemies were neighboring cities or barbarian tribes, whereas in August's time Rome was attacked by the great and ancient countries of the East; yet Vergil's description of the shield reveals the difference between the two periods to be one merely of degree, not of kind. The same virtues preserve both the republic and the empire, while the display of "barbaric" wealth by the Gauls and the Easteners alike suggests that avarice characterizes Rome's opponents in both periods. The republic's conflicts with its Italian neighbors result in the unified Italy which Augustus commands at the battle of Actium, and Rome's victory in that battle creates the unified empire which celebrates Augustus' triumph in the shield's closing scene. Analogously, in the first half of the chronicle barbarians such as those led by Humber and strife between members of the royal family pose the greatest threats to Britain, whereas in the second half Roman legions occupy Britain and hordes of Saxons invade after the Romans depart; yet Spenser's account reveals more similarities than differences between the two periods. The same virtues repeatedly rescue the kingdom throughout its history, and they are identical to the virtues which save Rome in its crises. Ambition characterizes Britain's bad rulers and its opponents in both periods of British history, as avarice marks

Rome's enemies; both vices are forms of intemperance in general and of greed--either for power or for wealth--in particular. Finally, the solution to the kinstrife of Brutus' line appears in Donwallo's unification of the island under a single strong central authority, and the times when Britain successfully resists Roman or Saxon occupation are those times when a strong king restores national unity. Vergil and Spenser agree that political unification permits the establishment of peace and the resumption of a civilized way of life.

As a whole, then, the chronicle teaches Arthur about both government and temperance, lessons equated by the definition of temperance as self-government. A good ruler possesses strength but wields it for the maintenance of peace. He settles and names lands, builds cities, gives laws, and shows religious reverence. Intemperance in the form of ambition poses the greatest threat to good governance by causing strife within the royal family, treason within the nation, overreaching on the part of the king himself. A good kingdom, like a healthy body, preserves itself by remaining united and repelling invaders; loss of its king or division of its regions causes its decay as surely as decapitation or dismemberment causes death for an individual.[36]

Furthermore, a ruler should love the country he governs. When Prince Arthur finishes reading the chronicle, his first speech indicates that his history lesson has inspired him with patriotism:

> Deare countrey, o how dearely deare
> Ought thy remembraunce, and perpetuall band
> Be to thy foster Childe, that from thy hand

> Did commun breath and nouriture receave?
> How brutish is it not to understand,
> How much to her we owe, that all us gave,
> That gave unto us all, what ever good we have.
>
> (x.69)

To understand that we owe our country gratitude for its nurturing us distinguishes us from the brute animals; all civilization presupposes such an elementary realization of common benefits and thence of community.[37] Thus the lessons taught by the chronicle and its effect upon the Prince both fit him for his future role as Britain's king.

Spenser has not permitted his readers to forget that Arthur will become a great and glorious monarch. After explaining how Caesar finally conquers the island, he comments that Rome oppressed the British "Till Arthur all that reckoning did defray" (x.49). This reference to Arthur's continental wars reminds the reader that Britain will enjoy its former reputation and will receive tribute once again rather than pay it out, thanks to Arthur's military prowess. Moreover, while speaking of Lucius' conversion to Christianity, Spenser adds:

> Yet true it is, that long before that day
> Hither came Joseph of Arimathy,
> Who brought with him the holy grayle, (they say)
> And preacht the truth, but since it greatly did decay.
>
> (x.53)

Mentioning the Grail recalls the fact that Arthur's reign will mark not only a return to secular power but also a renewal of spirituality. Arthur will both lead the Britons to worldly victory and inspire them to look beyond it to the imperishable glory of God.[38] Spenser's allusions keep Arthur's future kingship in our minds, so that the chronicle's role in fitting him for that kingship cannot escape us.

Just as Spenser alludes to Arthur's future, so that the reader sees
a greater purpose served by Arthur's reading the chronicle than he
himself did, so Vergil alluded to the future city of Rome during
Aeneas' tour of Pallanteum, so that the reader saw a greater purpose
served by Aeneas' visit to the site than he himself did. Indeed, a
total of three purposes are served in each case. Aeneas' visit to
Pallanteum prepares him for his immediate war with Turnus and Mezentius,
for his rule over both Trojans and Latins after the war, and for his
establishing the family which will, as Anchises prophesied in Aeneid
VI, produce Augustus. Arthur's reading the chronicle prepares him
for his immediate battle with Maleger, for his rule of Britain after
he returns from Faeryland, and for his restoring the greatness of the
royal line which will, as Merlin prophesies in III.iii, produce Elizabeth.

It remains necessary only to consider how Arthur's reading an
account of British history prepares him to fulfill his task in Canto
xi. The Prince challenges Maleger, the captain of the forces besieging
Alma's castle, to combat in order to lift the siege. Two hags,
Impotence and Impatience, assist Maleger, while Arthur is aided by
his squire, Timias. When Arthur engages Maleger in hand-to-hand combat,
he finds the captain very hard to kill. Piercing his body with a sword
opens up a bloodless wound, but does not slow Maleger down. Arthur

> doubted, least it were some magicall
> Illusion, that did beguile his sense,
> Or wandring ghost, that wanted funerall,
> Or aerie spirit under false pretence,
> Or hellish feend raysd up through divelish science.
> (xi.39)

Not easily discouraged, Arthur seizes Maleger and crushes him to death, casting his dead body down. Maleger bounds back to redouble his attack. Then the prince remembers that the Earth had borne Maleger "And raysd him up much stronger then before, / So soone as he unto her wombe did fall" (xi.45). Therefore Arthur strangles him in the air and carries him to a lake so that his corpse cannot touch the earth again. One of the twelve labors of Hercules was his slaying of the Libyan Antaeus, son of Neptune and Earth, in a similar fashion; Spenser's comparison of Arthur to Hercules recalls Vergil's comparison of Aeneas to Hercules in Aeneid VIII, and so increases the number of similarities between Arthur and Aeneas.[39]

Opinions as to Maleger's allegorical significance vary considerably. One may derive his name from male and aeger to make him "badly sick."[40] He appears "of such subtile substance and unsound, / That like a ghost he seem'd, whose grave-clothes were unbound" (xi.20). His use of a skull for a helmet heightens his resemblance to a corpse (xi.22). As Arthur notices, Maleger becomes "most strong in most infirmitee" (xi.40), as a bodily weakness does.[41] His assistants, Impatience and Impotence, represent conditions which both result from a state of illness (wherefore they follow Maleger's leadership) and make even a healthy body vulnerable to illness (wherefore they hand him weapons to aid his attack). We may conclude that, on one level, the threat Maleger poses to the castle of Alma is the danger disease presents to the human body.

Yet physical disease is both spiritual in origin, since it is one of the consequences of original sin, and spiritual in effect, since a sick person is less able to resist temptation.[42] Spenser's first descriptions of the castle of Alma and of Maleger suggest that as Alma represents good governance, so Maleger represents bad governance, which is another possible interpretation of his name (male and ger-, from gerere, "to govern"):[43]

> Of all Gods workes, which do this world adorne,
>   There is no one more faire and excellent,
>   Then is mans body both for powre and forme,
>   Whiles it is kept in sober government;
>   But none then it, more fowle and indecent,
>   Distempred through misrule and passions bace:
>   It growes a Monster, and incontinent
>   Doth loose his dignitie and native grace.
> Behold, who list, both one and other in this place.
>   (ix.1)

Spenser frequently describes allegorical characters in The Faerie Queene in terms which translate or gloss their proper names. Maleger, then, clearly represents both intemperance, the failure to govern oneself, as the term "Distempred" indicates, and "misrule," the failure to govern either oneself or others well. Throughout the British chronicle, Britain was threatened by intemperance and bad government. By defeating Maleger, Arthur demonstrates that he has learned the lessons which the chronicle had to offer. His victory symbolizes the assurance that he will be a good ruler, one who has conquered the temptations to be intemperate and to rule badly.[44]

Of course, on the literal level, Arthur perceives himself to be fighting a wily opponent on behalf of his gracious hostess, the governor of the beleaguered castle. The usefulness of his having read the chronicle is equally clear on this level. Much of the chronicle concerns the necessity of resisting attack by foreign forces, and

rulers need strength, wisdom, and loyal followers for successful
resistance. In offering to fight Maleger on Alma's behalf, Arthur
puts into practice what he has just learned about the importance of
defeating invaders. During his combat, he discovers that he, too,
must use his intelligence as well as his muscles in order to win.
Finally, Arthur himself would have lost the battle were it not for
Timias' faithful aid (xi.29-31). Arthur's ending the siege of Alma's
castle recalls various rulers' defense of Britain against Romans or
Saxons, who, like Maleger, were intemperate and unwise rulers, and
it anticipates his own defeat of the Saxons after his return to Britain
from Faeryland.

On the allegorical level, then, Arthur's visit to the castle
teaches him how to maintain a body and soul in good health, and he
applies this knowledge in order to defeat the physical disease and
spiritual intemperance which threaten one's health. On the literal
level, Arthur learns from Alma how to be a good castle governor and
removes for her the one external threat to her continued government.
The lessons taught in Canto ix remain the same whether we see their
example as a body or a castle, the governor as a soul or a lady. Both
for Arthur and for Spenser's readers, the British chronicle in Canto x
teaches the same lessons on a larger scale, with the body politic as
its example and kings as the ruling figures. To us, the applicability
of the castle's and the chronicle's lessons to Arthur's combat with
Maleger in Canto xi depends on our recognizing the captain as a repre-
sentation of illnesses of the body, the soul, and the body politic:

disease, intemperance, and misrule, respectively. To the prince, the historical account reveals both the importance of defeating Maleger and the means to use in doing so. Thus Arthur's visit to the castle of Alma and his reading the chronicle of British history prepare the Prince for his victory over Maleger, just as Aeneas' visit to the site of Rome and his receiving the shield engraved with scenes from Roman history prepared the Trojan general for his victories over Mezentius and Turnus.

Notes

[1] The chronicles' titles appear in II.ix.59-60.

[2] See the notes to II.x, Var. 2.301-03. Roche expresses the pre-vailing view, that the canto's purpose is to praise Queen Elizabeth by describing her royal predecessors and ancestors, in his notes to II.x, F.Q., p. 1129. Thomas H. Cain, Praise in The Faerie Queene (Lincoln: Univ. of Nebraska Press, 1978), devotes a chapter to "the encomiastic topos genus, or praise through descent" (p. 111), in which he includes both Gyuon's chronicle (pp. 114-15) and Arthur's (pp. 115, 118-20). I agree that both chronicles had an immediate political purpose, but I feel that they also both serve artistic purposes within the poem.

[3] The historical allegorists' interpretations appear in the notes to II.x.70 ff., Var. 2.334-38, and in the discussions by Katherine M. Buck, Kenneth T. Duffield, T. D. Kendrick, Isabel E. Rathborne, and Frances A. Yates, collectively titled "The Elfin Chronicle," Times Literary Supplement 47 (1948), pp. 79, 233, 275, 345, 359, and 373. The tendency to prefer Guyon's seven-stanza book to Arthur's sixty-four stanza book is not limited to the historical allegorists. For example, Thomas P. Roche, Jr., The Kindly Flame (Princeton: Princeton Univ. Press, 1964), discusses Guyon's chronicle for nine pages (pp. 34-42), but Arthur's chronicle for only two (pp. 43-44).

[4] Harry Berger, Jr., The Allegorical Temper, Yale Studies in English, Vol. 137 (New Haven: Yale Univ. Press, 1957; rpt. Archon Books, 1967), pp. 88-114.

[5] Critics have spilt much ink trying to guess how Spenser would have finished the poem, as may be seen in an appendix on "The Plan and Conduct of The Faerie Queene," Var. 1.314-62.

[6] Critics differ as to whether the attack is renewed only after Guyon leaves the castle because Spenser thought of Guyon as unable to deal with it or because the attackers thought of Guyon as too dangerous an opponent to face. For the former point of view, see Berger, pp. 50, 87-88, and 221-22; and A. C. Hamilton, "A Theological Reading of The Faerie Queene, Book II," English Literary History 25 (1958), 160-62. For the latter point of view, see Lewis H. Miller, Jr., "Arthur, Maleger, and History in the Allegorical Context," University of Toronto Quarterly 35 (1966), 176-78.

[7] Northrop Frye, Fables of Identity (New York: Harcourt, Brace & World, 1963), p. 77, defines the House of Holiness, the House of Alma, the Temple of Venus, and the Palace of Mercilla as "houses of

recognition." R. F. Hill, "Spenser's Allegorical 'Houses'," Modern Language Review 65 (1970), 722, includes sixteen of Spenser's sites in a complex classification of "static," "dynamic," "intermediate," and "mirror" allegory; the five sites I mention all appear in his intermediate category, "where the character(s) present are being tested by, instructed, or confirmed in, the values of the 'House' but without there being any dynamic tension of conflict." Angus Fletcher, The Prophetic Moment (Chicago: Univ. of Chicago Press, 1971), p. 12, claims that "The image of the temple is probably the dominant recurring archetype in The Faerie Queene. Major visions in each of the six books are presented as temples." Fletcher then lists the five sites I mention, plus the Garden of Adonis in Book III. Whether the Garden, which Spenser describes in Canto vi of Book III and which none of the knights in the poem visits, is equivalent to the other five sites is debatable.

[8] According to James Nohrnberg, The Analogy of The Faerie Queene (Princeton, N.J.: Princeton Univ. Press, 1976), p. 344, the three stages of the castle tour reveal the operation of "the natural, cordial, and animal spirits, which act on the body, the emotions, and the mind respectively." Berger, p. 72, describes the three parts of the castle as "the nutritive part of the vegetative power," "the appetitive part of the sensitive power," and "the apprehensive part of the sensitive power." Both schemes would have been familiar to Spenser.

[9] Critics differ as to the extent to which the two knights understand their encounters in the parlor. According to Hill, p. 731, "Guyon and Arthur experience a dramatic recognition of their true natures when confronted by Shamefastnesse and Praysdesire." Nohrnberg seems less confident about this episode's effect on Alma's guests: "these anima figures gently suggest the knights' limitations and perhaps qualify their self-estimates" (my italics; p. 345). Berger, p. 107, emphasizes the difference between the knights' reactions: "Arthur seeks more information. . . . Guyon seems to be made uncomfortable by the truth"; but he does not comment further on the extent to which they comprehend their experience. Kathleen Williams, Spenser's Faerie Queene (London: Routledge & Kegal Paul, 1966), p. 65, states firmly, "naturally enough, neither of the knights recognizes the thing he lives by."

[10] M. A. Manzalaoui, "The Struggle for the House of the Soul: Augustine and Spenser," Notes and Queries 206 (1961), 420-21, discusses the possibility that Spenser's description of memory as a chamber in the house of the soul derives from various phrases used by St. Augustine in Book X of the Confessions.

[11] Berger, p. 155, agrees that Spenser intended the literal and allegorical meanings of the castle to be given equal weight: "Alma's house is not an image yielding an idea, but two images confronting each other like the two parts of a simile; 'vehicle' and 'tenor' are castle occupants and body-soul; both are existants in the world of matter and spirit."

[12] The chronicle consists of 64 stanzas (x.5-68), so that the end of stanza 36 is its halfway mark. It is only in stanzas 37-39 that Spenser suggests that a new era has begun. Nevertheless, Berger proposes that Spenser's presentation of the historical events can be divided in two ways. One pattern results from the repeated interregna following a king's death without issue. These breaks in genealogical continuity occur at stanzas 36, 54, and 62, dividing the chronicle into four unequal sections. The second way Berger divides the chronicle is into two unequal parts, with the break occurring in stanza 50 when Spenser alludes to the Incarnation. Berger sees a qualitative difference in British history following the birth of Christ, and he sees that difference as being the main lesson of the chronicle. I completely disagree with this reading, although many of my interpretations of individual characters and specific events throughout the chronicle do coincide with Berger's.

[13] Carrie Anna Harper, The Sources of the British Chronicle History in Spenser's Faerie Queene (Philadelphia: John C. Winston, 1910), pp. 50-52. Harper's study of the relationship between Spenser's chronicle and its sources remains an invaluable work of scholarship, although she rarely offers any reason for Spenser's inventions, selection from alternative versions, and alterations.

[14] Harper, pp. 47-48.

[15] Berger fails to consider any event in the chronicle prior to Locrine's adultery. His omission of the first dozen stanzas from his discussion accounts in part for his unrelievedly negative judgment of Brutus' line.

[16] Brenda Thaon, "Spenser's British and Elfin Chronicles: A Reassessment," in Spenser and the Middle Ages, ed. David A. Richardson (Cleveland: Cleveland State Univ., 1976), p. 110.

[17] Berger, p. 112.

[18] Cain, p. 119, points out that Guendolene foreshadows Queen Elizabeth, an observation which suggests that he approves of Guendolene's actions. Williams does not mention Guendolene, but she includes Locrine in her list of negative exempla, p. 66. William Nelson, The Poetry of Edmund Spenser (New York: Columbia Univ. Press, 1963), p. 201, also condemns Locrine's behavior without commenting on Guendolene's.

[19] Harper, p. 63.

[20] Nelson, p. 201, condemns the brothers' conquest of Germany. Berger, p. 96, does not consider their deeds as important as their father's virility: Ebranck's twenty sons comprise less than half of

his children. Harper points out that Ebranck traditionally had either fifty or fifty-three children, but that Spenser assigns him fifty-two, "merely to substitute a poetical expression for the round number," p. 66. Berger makes much of the fact that Spenser has thereby related Ebranck and his offspring to the natural cycle of fifty-two weeks in a year.

[21] Berger, p. 96, condemns Brute's conquest of France.

[22] Bladud's death identifies him as a negative exemplum in the opinions of Thaon, pp. 114-15; Williams, p. 66; and Nelson, p. 201.

[23] Harper, pp. 83-84, observes that Spenser has no authority for Cordelia's hanging; in all previous versions of the story, she either kills herself by unspecified means or uses a knife. It seems likely that Shakespeare borrowed Cordelia's death by hanging from Spenser, although he made it murder rather than suicide.

[24] Berger, pp. 95, 90. Cain goes even further and calls the chronicle as a whole "dispiriting" (p. 114), "depressing" (p. 115), and "pessimistic" (p. 116). Michael O'Connell, Mirror and Veil (Chapel Hill: Univ. of North Carolina Press, 1977), pp. 77-78, firmly disagrees: "When we come to the end of the strife-filled account of Brutus's 'sacred progeny,' we almost suspect irony. . . . But it is more likely that such conflict is to be considered renowned and felicitous in an age of legendary heroes."

[25] The account of Brutus and his descendants occupies 27 stanzas (x.9-35). If Guendolene's revenge and rule are considered positive, then Spenser devoted 16½ stanzas to positive exempla and only 10½ to negative. If her deeds are considered negative, then Spenser maintained an exactly even balance between positive exempla (13½ stanzas, x.9-16, 21.6-26) and negative (13½ stanzas, x.17-21.5, 27-35). Any interpretation ought to take both sides seriously.

[26] O'Connell, p. 76, briefly compares Spenser's etymological explanations to those Evander gives Aeneas in the Aeneid, although the only specific "Vergilian precedent" he cites is that of Saturn's naming Latium. He also suggests that Spenser's giants resemble the fauns, nymphs, and men sprung from trees who inhabit Latium before Saturn gives them laws and names their land (Aen. 8.314-18).

[27] Harper, pp. 92-94, notes that traditional accounts of Donwallo's becoming king stress his use of violence and deceit.

[28] According to Harper, pp. 92-94, Spenser is the only writer to connect the crown of gold with the superiority of Donwallo's kind of kingship; other chroniclers merely report his wearing one or explain that he did so for richness of appearance, which is hardly an admirable motive.

[29] Harper, pp. 94-96.

[30] O'Connell, p. 78, observes, "It is significant that the first etymology Spenser gives in this section concerns law."

[31] Berger, pp. 94-96, disagrees, arguing that the age of Donwallo is wholly different from the age of Brutus with respect to the attributes of kingship.

[32] Berger, p. 98, calls Bunduca's story "a paradigm of the classical (especially the Stoic) doctrine of Temperance and its inadequacy." He admits, "Bunduca, the passage implies, was excellent [but] the Christian context around the passage implies a sharp rejoinder: Bunduca did not do the job." The "Christian context" consists of Spenser's references to the Incarnation (x.50) and to Joseph of Arimathea's coming to Britain with the Holy Grail (x.53). I do not feel that these stanzas justify reading all the subsequent stanzas in the chronicle as if they do not mean what they say. Cain, p. 119, claims that Bunduca "inevitably adumbrates Elizabeth." Certainly Spenser meant to imply no criticism of his queen. Finally, as O'Connell, p. 78, points out, "Bunduca will be held up to Britomart as a model of the woman warrior" (III.iii.54).

[33] In marked contrast to my interpretation of the interaction between Britain and Rome, Berger, p. 101, interprets the two intermarriages between Roman and British ruling families, the "Roman conquest" of the island, and the accession to the imperial purple of two British kings as "part of the Providential plan for maintaining and propagating man's freedom," part of "the engagement of Britain in a common history of the west." This reading is also based on Berger's tendency to interpret the events of the Christian era differently from the events preceding Christ's Incarnation; Berger concludes that Britain's "involvement" with Rome "embodies and carries forth the history of Christendom." I feel that Spenser's omission of Helena's and Constantine's contributions to the history of Christianity argues against this reading, as do Spenser's negative comments about Rome's motives and the disastrous results of all interaction between Rome and Britain.

[34] Harper, pp. 131-35.

[35] Williams, p. 66, reads the chronicle as a whole as being primarily a warning against "aspiration . . . the chief danger to temperance."

[36] Nelson, p. 200, relates the lessons of Cantos ix and x to each other in a similar fashion. Nohrnberg, p. 367, compares the image of "ordering power" presented by Alma to the positive exempla presented in the chronicle, and especially to Donwallo.

[37] Several critics can explain Arthur's reaction to the chronicle only by attributing to the Prince some perception which had not been

explicitly stated in the book he read. Thus Cain, p. 119, says that
Arthur's speech "seems unwarranted by [the chronicle's] dispiriting
nature unless we understand the exlamation as an intuition of Elizabeth."
Jerome S. Dees, "Notes on Spenser's Allegorical Structures," in Spenser
at Kalamazoo, ed. David A. Richardson (Cleveland: Cleveland State Univ.,
1978), p. 237, calls Arthur's response "an intuition of providential
order." Berger, p. 90, sees in "Arthur's unexpectedly optimistic
reaction . . . a perspective, born of humility, which reads deep into the
essential goodness of man's life in history, a goodness submerged
beneath so many tidal waves of violence and sedition."

[38] Berger does not discuss the association of the Grail with Arthur.
In his opinion, the important things to notice about stanza 53 are two:
that the truth preached by Joseph of Arimathea "did decay," an indication that the limitations of our mortal existence affect even the highest truth once it becomes incarnate, p. 97; and that Rome's military
conquest of Britain precedes the Grail's spiritual conquest, as
Arvirage's alliance with Rome precedes Lucius' alliance with Christianity, p. 100. It is from the fact that Britain's military and political
dealings with Rome precede the coming of Christianity to Britain that
Berger concludes that the earlier event was a prerequisite for the later
one, a conclusion which is not logically inevitable and which, as I have
often observed in these notes, leads to some questionable interpretations of the subsequent stanzas.

[39] A thorough and detailed discussion of the role of Hercules in
the Aeneid and in The Faerie Queene may be found in G. Karl Galinsky,
The Herakles Theme (Totowa, N.J.: Rowman and Littlefield, 1972), pp.
131-49, 206-12. Galinsky compares Vergil's and Spenser's allusions
to Hercules throughout his discussion of the English poem, observing
that Aeneas and Arthur are the primary figures linked with Hercules,
but not the only ones; that the linkage is accomplished by such means
as the parallels between Hercules' fight with Cacus and Aeneas' fight
with Turnus and those between Hercules' fight with Antaeus and Arthur's
fight with Maleger; and, in conclusion, that there is a "striking similarity between [Spenser's] associative, allusive technique and that
of Vergil," p. 212.

[40] Roche, note to xi.23.1, F.Q., p. 1135, following a note originally given by Child to xi.20 ff., Var. 2.343.

[41] Berger, p. 86, analyzes both Maleger's appearance and his
actions as "inversions generated from the notion of weakness as power."

[42] Var. 2.343, in Osgood's notes to xi.20-23. Critical interpretations of Maleger generally divide into three groups. One group of
critics sees Maleger simply as some sort of illness. Thus Cain, p.
99, identifies him as syphilis, and Frye, p. 81, and Nohrnberg, pp.
317-23, consider him to be the disease of melancholy. A second group

sees Maleger as original sin. Here belong Williams, p. 68, and Hamilton, p. 161. A third way to read Canto xi is to recognize the possibility that Spenser has left open both physical and spiritual meanings for Maleger. Thus Berger considers Maleger both as "unnatural melancholy," p. 85, and "Original Sin," p. 154, but concludes, "The qualities and acts of Maleger will not permit of any simple reduction; even his name is ambiguous," p. 155.

[43] Roche, in his note to xi.23.1, F.Q., p. 1135, suggests "'evil-bearer' (Latin: male, 'evil'; gerens, 'bearing')." Here he seems to be modifying a note originally given by Draper to xi.20 ff., Var. 2.343: "a coinage from the adverb 'male' and the verb 'gero,' to behave, i.e., evildoer." Professor Carter Revard proposed "to govern" or "to rule" as more precise translations of gerere. The English words gerent, "ruler," and vicegerent, "a ruler or commander of a country, etc., in virtue of deputed power," both appear for the first time in the 1500s, according to the O.E.D. Holinshed's Chronicles of England, Scotlande, and Irelande (1577), which Spenser clearly used repeatedly in Canto x's British history, is one of the sources of vicegerent, so Spenser was certainly familiar with the political meaning of the Latin verb gerere.

[44] To the best of my knowledge, no critic has considered a political interpretation of Maleger. However, Miller, alone among the critics I have read, does tie Arthur's combat to the chronicle in several particulars. He suggests that Maleger's gigantic size and earthly parentage recall the giants defeated by Brutus, pp. 183-84; that Spenser uses forms of the word swarm and comparisons to floods in describing both Maleger's forces and Humber's followers, in order to imply a parallel between Maleger and Humber, pp. 184-85; and that Arthur thinks of throwing Maleger into a lake partly because he has read of Locrine's drowning Humber in a river, p. 185. These points support my contention that Arthur's reading the chronicle prepares him for his combat with Maleger, a conclusion Miller also reaches.

Chapter 5

ARIOSTO AND TASSO

Spenser borrowed at least as heavily from Ariosto's <u>Orlando Furioso</u> and Tasso's <u>Gerusalemme Liberata</u> as from Vergil's <u>Aeneid</u>. He imitated words, names, phrases, items, characters, places, and entire episodes, always putting them to a markedly different use. For example, one of Ariosto's magicians has a crystal shield which dazzles all who behold it so greatly that they fall unconscious. The knight who acquires it considers it an unfair weapon and throws it down a well. When Spenser assigns Prince Arthur a shield with identical properties, however, it becomes a heavenly instrument which Arthur only employs against wicked and otherwise invincible foes. In similar ways, Spenser made everthing he borrowed his own property and part of an original work of literature. Often the result proves difficult to trace to its source, since Ariosto used Vergil's poem and Tasso used the works of both Ariosto and Vergil. Yet a close examination of the texts usually reveals the most likely primary model for a given passage by Spenser, even if details come from all three of his pre-decessors' works. The motif of encountering a man who has been trans-formed into a bush or tree, for instance, occurs in the <u>Aeneid</u>, <u>Orlando Furioso</u>, and <u>The Faerie Queene</u>. In each case, the hero of the poem damages the plant, it bleeds instead of oozing sap, and the voice of the transformed person emerges from the wound to tell his story. From such a general description, Vergil's and Ariosto's poems seem equally probable sources. But in the _Aeneid_, Aeneas learns that the plant houses the soul of a Trojan, murdered by his hosts for his gold and secretly buried where the tree now stands, whereas Ariosto's and Spenser's heroes discover that the plant holds a living man, transformed by a witch whom he had loved and who had grown tired of him. These additional details make it clear that Spenser followed Ariosto's work here more closely than Vergil's. In the remainder of this chapter, I shall consider the use of history in _Orlando Furioso_ and _Gerusalemme Liberata_, in order to determine the extent to which Arthur's chronicle and Merlin's prophecy derive from the Italian poems instead of or in addition to deriving from Vergil's _Aeneid_.

Ariosto's historical passages all occur in his subplot, which concerns Bradamante, a Christian warrior maid, and Ruggiero, a pagan warrior. These two fictional characters, like Britomart and Arthegall in _The Faerie Queene_, have historical descendants who include the poet's patron and ruler. Although they have met and fallen in love before the poem begins (II.32), the course of their true love runs very roughly indeed. Conflicting military as well as religious loyalties separate them; Bradamante serves Charlemagne, the emperor of Christendom, while Ruggiero serves Agramante, commander-in-chief of the pagan army attacking France. To further complicate matters, an enchanter named Atlante imprisons Ruggiero, whom he had raised and loves as a son (IV.30). Atlante knows that Ruggiero will convert to

Christianity and die shortly thereafter (IV.29); by keeping the warrior in captivity, Atlante hopes to prolong his life (IV.31).

Bradamante learns of Ruggiero's imprisonment and rides off to rescue him. En route, an envoy brings her word that a foreign army threatens Marseilles, whose defence Charlemagne had entrusted to her (II.62-64). Though briefly torn between love and duty, Bradamante decides to free Ruggiero before returning to the endangered city (II.65). Later the same day, she falls into a cave, off which a well-lit cavern opens. There a young woman greets her:

> O valiant Bradamante, not by chance,
> But in fulfilment of a will divine,
> You have arrived.
>
> (III.9)

She proceeds to tell Bradamante that this cavern contains Merlin's tomb, where his spirit dwells until the Last Judgment and whence his voice speaks to visitors (III.10-11). When Bradamante reaches the tomb, the dead magician's voice addresses her:

> May Fortune favour every wish of yours,
> O chaste and noble maiden, in whose womb
> The fertile seed predestined is to spring
> Which honour to all Italy will bring.
>
> (III.16)

Merlin then recalls Bradamante's Trojan ancestry and predicts her glorious descendants, including rulers, warriors, and princes who will renew the golden age (III.17-18). Finally, he assures her that Heaven has selected her to wed Ruggiero and implies that she made the right decision in postponing her return to Marseilles:

> By no consideration be deflected
> From what you now resolve, for, in your strife
> With the vile robber who your love immures,
> A speedy victory your fate ensures.
>
> (III.19)

Melissa, the enchantress who greeted Bradamante earlier, now conjures up spirits to assume the forms of the warrior maiden's descendants (III.20-23). Their description occupies thirty-six stanzas (III.24-59), eight of which describe Alfonso d'Este and his brother Ippolito, Ariosto's chief patrons. Melissa praises most of the Estensi for increasing the family's lands and titles and for defending Italy and the Church against their enemies, but she praises Alfonso just as warmly for defending himself against the papal and Venetian armies (III.51-55). After the enchantress dismisses the spirits, Bradamante asks about "two of grim, foreboding look" (III.60). Melissa turns pale, weeps, and addresses the unnamed pair as "victims both," misled by evil men (III.61). She also addresses Alfonso and Ippolito, pleading with them to have mercy on their erring kinsmen, before speaking to Bradamante:

> Let not this sadden you, I pray you.
> Of them I thought it wiser not to treat.
> So, leave the bitter and retain the sweet.
>
> (III.62)

Melissa thus gives her guest no clue as to the history of the grim-faced spirits, beyond indicating that they will err in some unspecified fashion. The prophecy ends on this vague but gloomy note.

Apparently Bradamante has lingering doubts about putting Ruggiero's freedom before Marseille's relief, but Merlin has none:

> The valiant Maid there tarried all the night
> And through the greater part of it conversed
> With Merlin, who convinced her it was right
> To put her duty to Ruggiero first.
>
> (III.64)

In the morning, she and Melissa depart together, so that the

enchantress can set her on the right road and tell her how to defeat
Atlante. Bradamante follows Melissa's directions and frees Ruggiero,
only to be separated from him again immediately when he mounts
Atlante's hippogriff and it flies away with him.

The winged horse, over which Ruggiero has no control, carries
him to an island in the West Indies. There Ruggiero becomes enamored
of the wicked sorceress, Alcina, who magically erases all his memories
of Bradamante (VII.16-18). Back in France, Melissa perceives
Ruggiero's situation and resolves to rescue him (VII.39-42). She
travels to Alcina's island, assumes Atlante's appearance, and waits
for an opportunity to see Ruggiero alone (VII.49-52). Soon he appears
in the garden, wearing silk clothes, a jeweled necklace, bracelets
on both arms, and pearl earrings, and with his hair curled and perfumed
(VII.53-55). Speaking in character as Atlante, Melissa reproaches
Ruggiero for his effeminacy (VII.56-59) and pleads with him on behalf
of his descendants:

> And if by thoughts of your own fame and by
> The noble deeds that are your destiny
> You are unmoved, then I will ask you why
> You have no scruple for your progeny,
> And to that womb how long you will deny
> The seed from which a glorious company
> Of offspring will descend, a mighty race,
> Destined in history to take its place?
>
> (VII.60)

From the family which Ruggiero will found, she singles out a familiar
pair to conclude her plea:

> Alfonso and Ippolito, who'll lead
> The world in virtue, and all good exceed.
>
> I told you of these brothers many a time
> And in my stories set them both apart,

> For in their valour they will be sublime.
> Of your descendants, they the greatest part
> Will have in chronicle and epic rhyme.
>
> (VII.62-63)

Her speech makes Ruggiero ashamed of himself, and Melissa promptly

slips a magic ring on his finger (VII.65). The ring dispels all

enchantments, so that Ruggiero ceases to regard Alcina with his former

infatuation immediately and sees both her and Melissa in their true

forms (VII.66-70). Alcina stands revealed as old, ugly, and decrepit,

a sight which effectively completes Ruggiero's cure (VI.71-74). He

escapes to the other side of the island, where a good enchantress,

Logistilla, supplies him with a bridle for the hippogriff and teaches

him how to control it (X.66-67).

Thanks to Logistilla's instruction, Ruggiero reaches France

safely, but he loses the winged horse almost as soon as he lands

(XI.13). Soon thereafter, he sees a giant defeat a knight, who lies

revealed as Bradamante when disarmed (XI.18-19). Ruggiero rushes to

her rescue, but the giant carries her away too quickly for the anxious

lover to catch up with them (XI.20-21). He follows the giant and

Bradamante into a palace, where he can find no trace of them (XII.17-18).

Whenever Ruggiero starts to leave, he hears his beloved calling him

and returns to search for her in vain (XII.19-20). Other warriors

fill the seemingly empty palace, each kept there by the perpetual

promise of what he most desires, an enchantment devised by Atlante

to trap both Ruggiero and his most valiant opponents (XII.21-22).

Meanwhile, the real Bradamante remains in Marseilles, where

Melissa brings her the news of Ruggiero's imprisonment (XIII.45-50).

The enchantress tells her how to break Atlante's spells and release
the knights he holds captive (XIII.51-53). As the two women travel
toward the palace together,

> Melissa used her skill
> The tedium of the journey to allay
> By pleasing converse as they made their way.
>
> Of all the themes the Maid rejoiced to hear,
> To one Melissa many times returned:
> The god-like progeny which she would bear
> In wedlock to the youth for whom she burned.
>
> (XIII.54-55)

Bradamante asks specifically whether her female descendants will
include any "valiant women" (XIII.56). In response, Melissa describes
several of the women who either descend from Bradamante or marry her
male descendants (XIII.57-73). As Alfonso received the most attention
in Melissa's previous prophecy, so his wife merits the longest
description here (XIII.69-71). The enchantress praises these women
for their virtue and for their excellence as wives and mothers, but
none of them does knightly deeds, as Bradamante seems to have hoped
they would.

Melissa leaves Bradamante before they reach Atlante's palace,
lest the enchanter recognize his professional rival (XIII.74-75).
Despite Melissa's repeated warnings, Bradamante immediately succumbs
to the same sort of deception as had ensnared her lover and the other
captive knights. Upon seeing two giants pursuing what seems to be
Ruggiero, the maiden charges after them, follows them through the
palace gates, and is caught in Atlante's trap (XIII.76-79). There
she and Ruggiero remain until Astolfo, an English duke equipped with
a magical horn and a book of magic, scatters the prisoners and destroys

the palace (XXII.16-23). Ruggiero and Bradamante, who fled in the same direction from the panic-causing horn, recognize each other as soon as it falls silent (XXII.31). After they finish celebrating their reunion and mourning the time they wasted in captivity, Bradamante tells Ruggiero that he must obtain her father's permission to marry her, having first converted to Christianity (XXII.32-34). Ruggiero agrees most willingly, and they set off to arrange for his christening.

Not surprisingly, a variety of adventures intervene, postponing Ruggiero's baptism and separating the lovers. Before they meet again, Bradamante receives another history lesson. In the castle where she has found shelter on a stormy night, frescoes depicting French invasions of Italy cover the walls, painted by demons under Merlin's direction (XXXIII.4-12). The castellan explains the paintings to Bradamante and his other guests at considerable length (XXXIII.13-57). Since the frescoes survey the thousand years between Merlin's time and Ariosto's, three centuries of which have already passed before the reign of Charlemagne, Bradamante views pictures of past events as well as of future ones. Generally, French monarchs who attempt to conquer Italy lose their armies either in battle or to disease, and some also lose their own lives, justly punished for their sins against the Italians and the Church. On the other hand, as the castellan carefully points out, Charlemagne and his father prospered in Italy because they came to defend the papacy:

> He points to Pepin and to Charlemagne,
> Showing how each to Italy descends,
> How each of them succeeds in his campaign,
> For neither harm to that fair land intends;

> But one against Aistulf the sovereign
> Pope Stephen aids; the other first defends
> Pope Adrian against the Lombard might,
> And next to Leo he restores his right.
>
> (XXXIII.16)

The castellan devotes more time to praising the deeds of Alfonso d'Avalos, one of Ariosto's secondary patrons, than he spends on any other figure or episode (XXXIII.27-30, 46-53). When he has concluded his description of the frescoes, his guests remain in the hall until bedtime, "fascinated at the future" (XXXIII.58).

Meanwhile, one crisis after another prevents Ruggiero from fulfilling his promise to convert to Christianity. On his way to Africa in the course of one adventure, he and the other passengers desert their storm-tossed ship, hoping to swim to a nearby island. In danger of drowning, Ruggiero realizes that his delays, however reasonable each seemed, had displeased God:

> Four times, ten times, in penitence he said,
> If God would overlook these sins so black,
> If ever he set foot on land again,
> He would become a Christian there and then.
>
> Never again would he use sword or lance
> Against the Faithful to support the Moor,
> But he would straight away return to France
> And render service to the Emperor.
> No longer would he lead his love a dance
> But as a husband honour her, he swore.
> O miracle! When he has promised this
> His strength and his agility increase.
>
> (XLI.48-49)

Upon reaching the island, Ruggiero finds it inhabited only by a hermit, to whom God has granted a vision not only of the knight's present arrival but also of his past, his future, and his offspring (XLI.52-54). The hermit instructs Ruggiero in the Christian faith, baptizes him the next day, and prophesies to him (XLI.55-60). This prophecy concentrates on Ruggiero's murder, the revenge Bradamante and his sister will take on the assassins, and the glorious character and deeds of his posthumous son (XLI.61-66). Only in one stanza does Ariosto allude to the hermit's describing all Ruggiero's descendants, including the Estensi: "Alfonso, unsurpassed, / And him to whom I dedicate my book," Ippolito (XLI.67).

Despite Ruggiero's conversion, various obstacles continue to prevent his marrying Bradamante for some time. As the wedding festivities finally begin, Melissa magically transfers the Byzantine emperor's pavilion to Paris for the happy couple's use (XLVI.77-79). The Trojan priestess, Cassandra, had embroidered this tent for Hector, and it has belonged in turn to Greek, Egyptian, Roman, and Byzantine rulers (XLVI.80-84). Cassandra had depicted in her embroidery Ippolito's life, virtues, and deeds, from his birth to the time of Ariosto's writing (XLVI.85-97). The newly wedded pair, unlike their guests, understand the pictures:

> Fair Bradamante was the only one
> To whom the sense had fully been made known.
>
> Ruggiero does not know the tale as well
> As Bradamante, but he calls to mind
> The stories which Atlante used to tell:
> Ippolito, whose glory he divined,
> He often praised.
>
> (XLVI.98-99)

With the tent's description, Ariosto's presentation of historical material in <u>Orlando Furioso</u> comes to an end.

Obviously, Spenser did not imitate certain features of Ariosto's

historical passages. Although Ariosto copied Anchises' Review of
Heroes by having Melissa summon spirits in the forms of Bradamante's
descendants, Spenser disregarded both examples and did not provide
Britomart with illustrations of Merlin's prophecy. Likewise, Melissa's
confrontation with Ruggiero in Alcina's garden echoes Mercury's appearance to Aeneas at Carthage, but Spenser wrote no such scene for any of
his heroes or heroines. Whereas Vergil covers the same period of
history in two passages, but emphasizes different aspects each time,
and Ariosto follows Vergil's example by having Melissa prophesy to
Bradamante in two speeches, covering the same family tree but describing only one gender at a time, Spenser's two historical passages do
not overlap chronologically at all. Moreover, since Spenser, like
Vergil, concentrates on public figures such as rulers and generals,
he never discusses the domestic virtues Melissa praises in her description of the female Estensi. Nor does Spenser present historical material
in works of art, such as the shield of Aeneas, the frescoes Bradamante
views, and the tent embroidered by Cassandra. (Admittedly, the chronicle which Arthur reads at the castle of Alma is an artifact, but a
verbal rather than a visual one.) Finally, Spenser does not give the
biography of Queen Elizabeth or any other historical character in the
way that Ariosto depicts the life of Ippolito on the embroidered tent.

On the other hand, Spenser clearly indicates his debt to Ariosto
by putting Merlin's prophecy in Canto iii of Book III, since Ariosto
had put the prophetic speeches of Merlin and Melissa in Canto III of
Orlando Furioso. Indeed, Spenser's choice of Merlin to deliver the

prophecy to Britomart may have owed something to Ariosto's use of the
magician, though the decision to set The Faerie Queene in Arthur's
youth made it inevitable that Merlin should appear in the poem in
some capacity. More importantly, Ariosto apparently gave Spenser the
idea of explaining the relationship between fortune and divinely
ordained fate. Just as Melissa tells Bradamante that she fell into
Merlin's cave "not by chance, / But in fulfillment of a will divine"
(O.F. III.9), so Merlin informs Britomart that she saw Arthegall in
the mirror not by accident but on account of "eternall providence,
that has / Guided thy glaunce, to bring his will to pas" (F.Q. III.
iii.24). Furthermore, Spenser assigns to his Merlin a very close
copy of the only speech Merlin makes in Orlando Furioso. Both Ariosto's
original and Spenser's adaptation occupy three and one-half stanzas.
In Ariosto's poem, the magician's voice addresses Bradamante, "in
whose womb / The fertile seed predestined is to spring," recalls her
Trojan ancestry, predicts her valiant descendants, who will restore
Italy, and reassures her about her current quest to release Ruggiero
from captivity (O.F. III.16-19). Similarly, in The Faerie Queene,
Merlin says to Britomart, "from thy womb a famous Progenie / Shall
spring," and proceeds to recall her Trojan ancestry, predict her
valiant descendants, who will restore Britain, and reassure her about
her current quest to find Arthegall (F.Q. III.iii.21-24). The final
parallel between the two scenes occurs at the end of the prophecies.
In the Aeneid, the Review of Heroes concludes with Anchises' lament
for the untimely death of young Marcellus, a cause for sorrow which

Anchises fully explains to Aeneas. But in <u>Orlando Furioso</u>, when
Melissa grieves over the erring kinsmen of Alfonso and Ippolito, she
does not tell Bradamante anything about their deeds. Bradamante must
recover from the distress caused by Melissa's outburst without even
understanding the reason for that outburst. Likewise, Britomart sees
Merlin fall into a fit of what seems dismay after saying, "But yet the
end is not," and never discovers what caused his dismay. All three
prophecies thus end in momentary unhappiness, but Spenser follows
Ariosto's example rather than Vergil's in not having the prophet explain
the reason for that unhappiness to the listening character.

In each of these cases of Ariostan influence, Spenser expands
the borrowed material for his own purposes. In <u>The Faerie Queene</u>,
Merlin discusses fortune, fate, predestination, and free will, answer-
ing Glauce's questions about their relationship and correcting miscon-
ceptions which the nurse and Britomart had shared. Although Melissa's
greeting to Bradamante in <u>Orlando Furioso</u> seems to have suggested this
topic, Ariosto did not develop it beyond the one sentence quoted above,
nor had Bradamante shown any sign of needing instruction in it. Even
in Merlin's speech, where Spenser follows Ariosto very faithfully, the
English poet has caused his source's "fertile seed" to grow into a
"Tree, / [With] big embodied braunches." Finally, Spenser goes one
step further than Ariosto in obscuring the end of the prophecy. While
Melissa's allusions to the two unfortunate Estensi she does not name
remain mysterious to Bradamante, Ariosto's readers had no trouble
recognizing the pair and remembering their story. But Spenser's readers

had no more idea than did Britomart what "ghastly spectacle" Merlin foresaw when he stopped speaking.

Two of Ariosto's other passages evidently contributed to Merlin's prophecy in The Faerie Queene. Neither the second prophecy Melissa delivers to Bradamante nor the one which the hermit gives Ruggiero is illustrated by spirits, a fact which may have influenced Spenser's decision not to have Merlin display Britomart's descendants in visible form. The hermit's prediction had another, more specific contribution to make: his description of Ruggiero's murder and his posthumous son clearly served as the model for Merlin's predictions regarding Arthegall and his posthumous son. Here, however, Spenser has condensed rather than expanded his source, so that nothing of Ariosto's story remains except the hero's treacherous assassination followed by the birth of a child whose duplication of his father's glorious character and deeds will comfort his bereaved mother.

The chronicle in Book II of The Faerie Queene probably also owes something to Ariosto's example. Bradamante reviews previous historical events as well as learning of future ones by looking at the frescoes, so that Spenser had a precedent in Orlando Furioso for educating his hero in his country's past history. Yet Spenser could as easily have gotten this idea from Aeneas' exposure to the Latin past in Aeneid VIII. A second area of possible Ariostan influence concerns the subject matter of the chronicle, which presents a chronological record of the nation's history rather than a genealogical account of the hero's family. Ariosto's description of the

frescoes constitutes the only historical passage in his poem which
does not praise the Estensi and which does exhibit national instead
of familial pride. Again, however, Vergil supplied both poets with
a model by describing the history of Rome rather than the descendants
of Aeneas on the shield in _Aeneid_ VIII. Only the third and last
suggestion Spenser could have found in _Orlando Furioso_ does not appear
also in the _Aeneid_. Aristo states that both the frescoes and the
embroidered tent feature sufficient lettering to identify their
figures and scenes, thus making these works of art verbally as well
as visually instructive. That mixture of forms provides an intermediate step between the purely visual engravings on Aeneas' shield
and the purely verbal chronicle in _The Faerie Queene_.

Despite Spenser's many and various debts to Ariosto, his use
of historical material remains Vergilian in one important respect:
its effect on the character exposed to it. In _Orlando Furioso_,
Bradamante learns of her male descendants after she has decided to
put Ruggiero's rescue ahead of Marseilles' defense, and of her
female descendants as she travels to his aid on a later occasion.
Merlin does assure her that she has made the right decision, but
neither his speech nor either of Melissa's prophecies affects the
warrior maiden's character or influences her behavior. Indeed,
Ariosto admits that Melissa predicts the Estensi women solely "The
tedium of the journey to allay" (_O.F._ XIII.54). Melissa's confrontation with Ruggiero, like Mercury's appearance to Aeneas, recalls
prophecies formerly given to the hero, but Ariosto, unlike Vergil,

has not previously shown the reader the delivery of such prophecies,
so that Melissa's reference lacks the impact of its classical model.
The frescoes apparently serve only as a diversion for Bradamante
and her fellow guests at a castle one night; their moral, that the
French ought not to invade Italy, does not apply to the Carolingian
period, as the castellan points out. By the time Ruggiero receives
a prophecy from the hermit, he has already accepted baptism and
committed himself to fight for Christendom against his former overlord.
Finally, the biographical tent appears during the celebration of
Bradamante and Ruggiero's wedding, simply to add to the festivities.
Ariosto evidently uses history either to entertain his characters
or to reward them for right actions, but not to instruct or motivate
them; his historical material may change his readers, but it does not
affect his hero and heroine in the way that Vergil's and Spenser's
passages affect theirs.

Tasso's historical passages both occur in the story of Rinaldo,
one of his poem's two heroes. Since Rinaldo, one of the best warriors
among the Crusaders, has been gone from the Christian camp for some
time, the commander-in-chief sends two knights, Charles and Ubaldo,
to recall him (XIV.27-28). Peter the Hermit directs the knights to
ignore the suggestions Rinaldo's uncle has made as to his nephew's
whereabouts and tells them to consult another hermit for more accurate
information (XIV.29-31). Charles and Ubaldo take Peter's advice, find
the hermit, and learn from him what has happened to Rinaldo. A Saracen

enchantress, Armida, cast him into an enchanted sleep in order to kill him, but then fell in love with him and abducted him to one of the Fortunate Islands, where they remain bound together by mutual love (XIV.57-71). The hermit promises his guests a boat with a pilot, a wand to frighten away Armida's guardian monsters, a map of the maze in which she has imprisoned Rinaldo, and an adamantine shield to show Rinaldo himself in (XIV.72-77). The boat, wand, and map all perform as promised. Upon reaching a marvellous garden at the center of the maze, Charles and Ubaldo find Rinaldo and Armida lying together on the grass, and they discreetly bide their time behind a bush (XVI.17-19). As soon as the enchantress leaves her lover, the knights reveal themselves to Rinaldo, who finds their warlike appearance immediately arousing (XVI.28-29). When Ubaldo holds up the shield of adamant to Rinaldo,

> he in that mirror sees himself at once,
> effeminately groomed, his hair, his cloak
> beribboned, fragrant with lascivious smell.
>
> (XVI.30)

Overcome with shame, Rinaldo cannot bear to look either at himself or at his former comrades (XVI.31). Ubaldo briefly rebukes him for his inactivity, citing religion, glory, and duty as reasons for Rinaldo to return (XVI.32-33). This speech quickly has the desired effect on the hero:

> and when a higher, more consuming flame
> follows the flush that covers all his face,
> he tears his rich dress off, off all those lewd
> ornaments, symbols of cheap servitude.
>
> Burning for his departure, right away
> he leaves the complex, labyrinthine paths.
>
> (XVI.34-35)

The three knights leave the island together, undeterred by Armida's following Rinaldo and pleading with him at the ocean's edge (XVI.40-62).

Landing in Palestine at night, they see a glimmering gold and silver light, which turns out to come from a suit of armor, a helmet, and a shield (XVII.57-58). They find the hermit guarding these items and waiting to give Rinaldo a lecture on the superiority of virtue to pleasure and of reason to wrath (XVII.59-63). Since Rinaldo's hot temper had caused him to leave the Christian camp and his liaison with Armida had delayed his return, the hermit's speech makes a deep impression on him (XVII.64). The hermit then shows Rinaldo the shield, engraved with the great deeds of his noble ancestors, and spurs the hero into action with these words:

> Oh, you are still behind them all, and seem
> to move quite slowly in this glorious race.
> Up! Up! Rise fast! and let the feats I show
> arouse and hasten your still dormant worth.
> (XVII.65)

Tasso describes the engravings, which cover the centuries between the fall of the Roman Empire and the First Crusade, without any overt allusions to events later than Rinaldo's lifetime. Nevertheless, his references to Este and to the Guelphs (XVII.67, 70-72, 79-81) remind his readers that the Estean and Guelphic ruling families of the sixteenth century claim Rinaldo as their common ancestor. The poet praises his patrons' distant forebears for their valor, piety, and acquisition of increasing territory and wealth. He admits that several of the family's warriors have died in battle, but rejoices in the glory that they won rather than grieving for their deaths.

Rinaldo finds that the sight of his ancestors' deeds inspires him

to emulate them:

> His proud soul burned with envy, and so much
> the vision of that glory fired his mind
> that in his every thought, right now, right now,
> he won and captured towns, and slaughtered foes.
> (XVII.82)

Delighted at the effect of his gift, the hermit conveys the three

knights back to their camp.

On their way, the hermit apologizes for his lack of prophetic

ability (XVII.87-88). Fortunately for Rinaldo, however, the hermit

has often heard the future prophesied by a friend of his and can

recall that Rinaldo's descendants will include a great number of

heroic figures (XVII.89). Chief among them will be Alfonse II of

Este, Tasso's primary patron, whom the hermit praises for his acts

both in war and in peace and who he hopes will declare a new crusade

against Islam (XVII.90-94). This revelation completes Rinaldo's

instruction by the hermit and Tasso's presentation of historical

material.

Tasso goes one step further than Ariosto in removing historical

references from the scene in which his hero is recalled to the path

of duty. In the _Aeneid_, Mercury reminded Aeneas of prophecies and

divine commands which the reader had seen Aeneas receiving; in

Orlando Furioso, Melissa reminded Ruggiero of his prophesied descendants,

although the reader had not known that Ruggiero had any prior knowledge

of them; but in _Gerusalemme Liberata_, Ubaldo simply reminds Rinaldo

of the current state of affairs. On the other hand, Tasso does
indicate that the shield completes the process of renewing Rinaldo's
commitment to his religious and military duty. As Rinaldo's first
reaction to seeing himself in Ubaldo's shield of adamant--"Down
falls his glance, and, timid and ashamed, / he keeps it bent upon the
ground" (XVI.31)--gave way to "a higher, more consuming flame"
(XVI.34), so his demeanor during the hermit's lecture--"meek and sad,
/ he kept his shameful glance bent on the ground" (XVII.64)--gives
way to his soul's being fired by the vision of his ancestors' glory
(XVII.82). By paraphrasing Vergil's description of Aeneas' response
to the Review of Heroes, Tasso pays homage to his model for this use
of history. The relationship between the confrontation in Armida's
garden and the shield of Rinaldo is exactly analogous to the relationship between the confrontation at Carthage and the Review of Heroes.
However, Tasso follows Ariosto's example rather than Vergil's at
the end of the canto. The hermit's prediction of Alfonso II recalls
the prophecies delivered to Bradamante and Ruggiero by Melissa and
the hermit in being given as a reward for making the right decision.
The passage also seems more Ariostan than Vergilian in its biographical
detail, and it shares with the shield's engravings an emphasis on clan
rather than country, an emphasis common in Ariosto's work but almost
unknown in Vergil's.

Obviously, Spenser could have borrowed the use of history to
effect character change as easily from the function of Rinaldo's
shield as from the function of Anchises' prophecy. He could likewise

have borrowed the hero's exposure to the past as easily from the
subject matter of Rinaldo's shield as from the history Aeneas learns
at the site of Rome. But Tasso has combined these elements, present
in all three works, in one passage, and both Vergil and Spenser kept
them separate. Tasso borrowed the hero's exposure to the past from
Aeneas' visit to Pallanteum and assigned to it the function of
Anchises' prophecy. Spenser, like Vergil, uses a genealogical
prophecy to effect character change in one passage, while exposing
his hero to the past for a different purpose in a different book of
his poem. As a result, Spenser can imitate more aspects of Vergil's
use of history than Tasso can in his briefer presentation. For
example, Vergil and Spenser both use revelations of future events to
effect character change, in contrast to Tasso's using a revelation
of past events for that purpose. Also, Vergil and Spenser arrange
for their heroes to learn about the past not in order to affect
their characters but to prepare them for combat by showing them the
necessity of defeating their opponents. Rinaldo learns no analogous
lesson because Tasso takes the necessity of Christians conquering
Saracens for granted. It seems far more likely, then, that Spenser
found the inspiration for his use of history in the Aeneid than
in Gerusalemme Liberata.

In summary, Spenser borrows extensively from Ariosto in detail,
but uses these borrowed details in a Vergilian manner. Orlando
Furioso probably influenced the form of both historical passages in
The Faerie Queene: the lettered labels on the frescoes and the tent

suggested conveying history by means of a literary work, such as the
chronicle, and the absence of spirits from two of the Ariostan
prophecies provided a precedent for Spenser's omitting them from
his. Ariosto also supplied Spenser's prophetic passage with much
of its content: a distinction between fortune and fate; a speech by
Merlin about the heroine's Trojan ancestry, glorious progeny, and
current plight; the assassination of the heroine's beloved after a
fairly short marriage; the birth of a posthumous son; and an unhappy
ending which the prophetic figure leaves unexplained. On the other
hand, Ariosto does not use historical material either to motivate his
characters and change their attitudes or to prepare them for coming
conflicts, the two purposes to which Vergil and Spenser both put
history in their poems. Tasso does use the engravings on Rinaldo's
shield to complete a process of character change, but in doing so he
combines the form of one Vergilian passage with the function of
another. Since Spenser's two historical passages correspond more
nearly both in form and in function to Vergil's two than they do to
Tasso's one, presumably Spenser imitated Vergil. Finally, a sense
of national destiny pervades all the historical material in the _Aeneid_
and _The Faerie Queene_, but does not appear in the Italian poems.
Despite many specific borrowings, therefore, Spenser's use of history
remains primarily Vergilian in form, function, and theme.

CONCLUSION

In The Faerie Queene, Spenser borrowed several aspects of
Vergil's use of history in the Aeneid. The historical passages in
The Faerie Queene II and III resemble those in Aeneid VI and VIII
in both form and theme to a certain extent, but the closest parallels
between the two works involve the function of the historical revelations in terms of their effect on the characters who receive them.
In all three respects, Merlin's prophecy in Faerie Queene III follows
the example set by Anchises' prophecy in Aeneid VI, while Arthur's
exposure to the castle of Alma and the chronicle in Faerie Queene II
imitates Aeneas' exposure to the site of Rome and the shield in
Aeneid VIII.

In the Aeneid, Aeneas struggles against his destiny in various
ways throughout Books I-IV. Three episodes turn him into the fully
committed and confident leader of Books IX-XII. First, in Aeneid
IV, Mercury confronts him at Carthage with Jupiter's command to cease
postponing the destined settlement in Italy. Mercury refers to the
prophecies which Aeneas has received in Books II-III, so that his
rebuke comes not as an isolated event but as the culmination of a
process. Aeneas has seen ghostly images of human Hector and Creusa,
heard mortal priests at Delos and Buthrotum deliver divinely inspired
messages, and had a vision in his sleep of his familiar household gods,

but now he sees one of the Olympians face to face, while fully awake.
As a result, he finally accepts his destiny to an unprecedented
extent. Mercury's speech convinces Aeneas that he can and will
find a new home, which he had often despaired of doing. By referring
to the settlement as "Roman," Mercury gives Aeneas the first indication that his new home will differ in name, and therefore presumably
in nature, from his former city. Finally, the god's personal appearance teaches Aeneas that the Olympians take a great interest in his
mission and that his actions have some purpose in their plans for
human history. This confrontation thus replaces Aeneas' despair
with hope, begins correcting his misunderstanding of the nature of
his task, and informs him of his destiny's importance to the gods.

In _Faerie Queene_ III, Britomart goes through a much shorter but
analogous process. When she falls in love with Arthegall's image in
the magic mirror, she does not accept her emotion as her destiny
but struggles against it. She suffers from shame, because she fears
her lover unattainable. Glauce, in Canto ii, dispels the princess'
shame by teaching her to distinguish between abnormal desire and normal
love at first sight, which she sees as Britomart's condition. Furthermore, the nurse convinces Britomart that Arthegall may prove attainable, since his image could not appear unless he really existed. In
order to learn Arthegall's whereabouts, the two women visit Merlin's
cave in Canto iii. The magician assures Britomart that loving
Arthegall is her duty and marrying him her fate. He also reveals to
her that God ordains the course of human history and that her marriage
has a role to play in the divine plan. Between them, then, Glauce

and Merlin replace Britomart's despair with hope, correct her misunderstanding of the nature of her emotion, and inform her of her destiny's
importance to God. The stage of her progress from lovesick damsel
to love-inspired warrior at which she hears Merlin's prophecy of her
descendants thus corresponds to the stage of Aeneas' progress from
reluctant and inadequate obedience to eager and complete commitment
at which he hears Anchises' prophecy of his descendants.

Aeneas' experiences in Aeneid VI constitute the second formative
episode in his development and complete his commitment to his task.
This episode has two parts, the first of which has no analogy in
The Faerie Queene. Because Aeneas needs to renounce his previous
commitments to fallen Troy, to the many ill-chosen sites of attempted
settlement during his years of wandering, and to Carthage and its
queen, he encounters the shades of his former comrade, his helmsman,
and his beloved. He must leave each of them behind in order to
proceed to see Anchises and learn about the future, which he must
love instead of the past they represent. Each helps send him forward
on his appointed path, the men by what they say and Dido by her
refusal to speak. Then Aeneas comes to the shade of Anchises in the
Elysian Fields and views with him the souls of their descendants.

Anchises' prophecy divides into two sections of approximately
equal length, plus an epilogue. In the first section, Anchises
condenses a vast stretch of history in order to bring Augustus into
closer proximity with the first few generations after Aeneas than an
unabridged account would permit. This section emphasizes genealogical

continuity and the activities of settling lands, naming places, and founding communities. It concludes with a description of the peace which Augustus will establish universally, after which Anchises asks Aeneas whether he can now continue entertaining either doubts or fears about his destiny. The descendants described in this section offer Aeneas models for his own task of founding and naming a settlement for his followers, and both the continuity of his line and its eventual establishment of a harmonious empire give him causes for confidence and pride. In the second section, Anchises recounts the deeds of a large number of historical figures, mostly noteworthy for governmental or military achievements. By presenting these figures out of chronological order, Vergil juxtaposes the unhappy but patriotic Brutus with happier patriots and the self-serving Caesar and Pompey, whose enmity hurts their country, with various self-sacrificing generals whose valor brings glory both to their country and to themselves. This arrangement teaches Aeneas that service to Rome matters more than personal happiness, and the conclusion of the section explains why that should be true. Anchises reveals that Rome has a great civilizing mission, to use its governmental and military expertise to give laws, make peace, protect suppliants, and "wear down the proud with war" (debellare superbos, 6.853). After that magnificently inspiring speech, the prophecy ends on the sad note of Anchises' mourning for the untimely death of his most promising descendant, Augustus' heir. Despite the sad ending, however, the Review of Heroes has the desired effect on Aeneas. Anchises has

"kindled his soul with love of the glory to come" (<u>incendit</u> . . .
<u>animum famae venientis amore</u>, 6.889), and this inspiration completes
the process of committing Aeneas to his destiny.

Since Britomart has no previous commitments to renounce when
she falls in love with Arthegall, there exists in <u>The Faerie Queene</u>
no analogy to Aeneas' experiences in the first half of <u>Aeneid</u> VI.
The parallels between Aeneas' situation and Britomart's resume when
Merlin begins to prophesy Britomart's descendants. His prophecy
divides into two sections of unequal length, after which it breaks
off abruptly. In the first section, Merlin recounts the deeds of a
large number of figures, mostly noteworthy for governmental or
military achievements. By altering historical tradition at several
points, Spenser first creates a pattern of arbitrarily alternating
success and failure and then reveals God's intervention in history
to punish the wicked and avenge the innocent. This arrangement
teaches Britomart that doing God's will matters more than personal
happiness. In the second section, Merlin condenses a vast stretch
of history in order to bring Elizabeth Tudor into closer proximity
with the first few generations after Britomart than an unabridged
account would permit. This section emphasizes genealogical continuity and the continuation of virtue and valor, love and courage, in
Britomart's descendants. It concludes with a description of the
peace which the Tudor rulers will establish throughout the British
Isles. The figures described in this section offer Britomart models
for her own courageous quest to fulfill her love, and both the

continuity of her line and its eventual establishment of a harmonious

nation give her causes for confidence and pride. Merlin does not

hesitate to admit that Elizabeth will need to continue exercising

military power, however; Spenser undoubtedly considered the protection

of Belgium and the defeat of the Spanish Armada, which Merlin alludes

to in the last stanza of his speech, as England's equivalents of Rome's

mission to protect suppliants and wear down the proud with war.

After that inspiring description, which Britomart undoubtedly found

all the more attractive for its featuring a royal virgin like herself,

the prophecy ends with Merlin's abrupt silence and dismayed looks.

Yet despite its sad ending, the historical revelation has the desired

effect on Britomart. When Glauce suggests that the princess don arms

to search for Arthegall, Britomart responds with "great desire" and

"generous stout courage" (iii.57), because Merlin's prophecy has

completed the process of committing her to her destiny.

Aeneas' experiences in Aeneid VIII form the third and last

episode which prepares him for the events of Books IX-XII. Already

completely committed to settling in Latium when Book VIII opens,

Aeneas finds it disturbing that he must begin by fighting Turnus

and his allies. In the course of the book, two occurrences give

him the knowledge and confidence to accept the necessity of combat.

First, Aeneas visits Pallanteum, a community of Arcadian exiles on

the site of Rome. There he hears the story of Hercules' combat with

Cacus, a monster infamous for his savage slaughter of neighboring

men. The Arcadian king, Evander, also tells Aeneas the history of

Latium in an account which stresses the contrast between good rulers, who govern peacefully, make laws, build cities, and give names to places, and bad rulers, who indulge their violent and avaricious impulses and change the settled names of places. Finally, Evander gives Aeneas a tour of Pallanteum and advises him to eschew pride and greed in favor of Hercules' humility and the austerity of the Arcadians' way of life. Both the tale of Hercules and the history of Latium teach Aeneas that a leader must be willing to use violent means to quell the violence of characters like Cacus and Turnus. Thus the hero's exposure to the past prepares him for the battle he must fight in the immediate future. Moreover, Evander's advice to be temperate teaches Aeneas about self-government; the examples of good and bad rulership show him how to govern well after winning the war; and the information he gains about his new country, its history, and its religious customs will likewise prove useful in his future rule over Latins as well as Trojans. Aeneas' history lessons, then, prepare him for his eventual kingship as well as for his forthcoming combat.

In *The Faerie Queene* II.x, Arthur reads a chronicle of British history which sets forth the same themes and serves the same purposes as Aeneas' visit to Pallanteum. The chronicle contains numerous examples of good rulers, who govern peacefully, make laws, build cities, name places, and defeat violent giants, rebels, and invaders; and of bad rulers, who indulge their violent and ambitious impulses and change the settled names of places. In II.xi, Arthur fights Maleger, whose violent attack on Alma's castle presents a threat very much like that presented by many of the characters in the chronicle. On the allegorical level, Maleger represents not only the political phenomenon of misrule, as indicated by his name, but also the individual vice of intemperance, or ill-governance of the self, which causes a ruler to govern others badly. Arthur's reading the chronicle prepares him to defeat Maleger on both levels, by teaching him the necessity of using force to quell the violence of lawless opponents and by showing him the qualities which a wise ruler exercises in order to overcome his own natural tendencies to intemperance. In addition, the chronicle prepares Arthur to rule Britain after returning from Faeryland by teaching him how to govern wisely and by inspiring him with patriotic feelings toward the country he will rule. Thus the hero's exposure to the past makes him ready for his eventual kingship as well as for his immediate combat.

The last incident in Aeneid VIII consists of Venus' bringing Aeneas the arms Vulcan has made, which include a shield engraved with scenes from Roman history. This gift of magical armor and weapons completes the restoration of Aeneas' confidence with regard to fighting and winning his war with Turnus. Although Aeneas does not fully comprehend the pictures on his shield, the reader realizes that they present the same images of rulership and moral lessons that Aeneas had learned at Pallanteum: respect for law, contempt for wealth, the qualities of a good ruler, and the necessity of opposing violence with force in order to establish peace. The shield's engravings, described in chronological order, also show that the history of Rome has two stages. In the first, threats to the city come from other Italian communities or from barbarian invaders, but eventually a unified Italy results from the centuries of conflict. At the battle of Actium, as Rome enters a new era by acquiring an empire, the danger to recently unified Italy comes from the hetero-genous forces of the East, but Augustus' triumph afterwards shows that the diverse countries of the empire can unite under Rome's leadership as harmoniously as had the Italian city-states. In receiving the shield, Aeneas acquires symbolic possession of the historical process it portrays and thereby completes his preparation for the coming combat; his own war will result in the union of Latins and Trojans, whose descendants will become the Romans who will unify first Italy and then all the known world.

The chronicle Arthur reads shows that British history likewise has two stages. In the first, threats to the kingdom come from internal strife or from barbarian invaders, but eventually Donwallo unifies the island and rules peacefully. During the succeeding centuries, the danger to Britain comes primarily from the forces of Rome, but the Britons resist successfully whenever they unite. The chronicle repeatedly shows the perils of disunity and the fruits of renewed national union. For Britain, as for Rome, internal peace and external power result from the political unity which only a strong central authority can provide. This political truth also appears in Canto ix of Book II, in the castle of Alma. Its internal peace and the strength to resist external threats such as Maleger's derive

from the authority Alma exercises over her household. As Alma's
guest, Arthur sees the same lessons about government taught by the
way she runs her castle as he subsequently learns from reading the
chronicle. On the allegorical level, the castle represents a human
body; the ladies in its parlor, the heart's passions; and Alma's
counsellors, the faculties of the mind. All obey the strong central
authority of Alma, who represents the soul. Her wise rule over her
physical, emotional, and intellectual subjects illustrates the virtues
of temperance, or good self-government, and results in a peaceful life
and the strength to resist temptations such as Maleger's followers
represent. Although Arthur does n ot fully comprehend the nature of
Alma's castle, the reader realizes that the allegorical artifact
teaches the same lessons as the historical chronicle. Spenser, like
Vergil, educates his hero in ways not completely perceived by that
hero but ensures the character's comprehension of all the necessary
lessons by presenting them also in more explicit forms.

In conclusion, Spenser imitates Vergil's use of history in
several ways. Merlin's prophecy resembles Anchises' prophecy very
closely, having a bipartite form, using analogous techniques to
make historical material illustrate moral truths, presenting models
among the listening character's descendants for that character's
own actions, praising the poet's patron and ruler, ending on an
unhappy note, and completing the process of committing the listening
character to cooperation with a divinely ordained destiny. Arthur's
experiences in The Faerie Queene II have a more complex relationship

to Aeneas' experiences in <u>Aeneid</u> VIII. Both heroes learn from
explicit accounts of the past lessons which prepare them for immediately necessary combat and for eventual kingship. Alma's castle
presents these lessons allegorically and Aeneas' shield displays
them in a form which Aeneas can only grasp symbolically. Thus the
site of Rome, the shield of Aeneas, the castle of Alma, and the
chronicle of Arthur all teach the same truths, but in different modes
and with different examples. Not surprisingly, Vergil and Spenser
praised moral government, national unity, peace when possible, and
strength when necessary, in all four of their historical passages;
even though history never exactly repeats itself, the political
benefits of Elizabeth's reign recalled those of Augustus' rule in
many ways, and the poets remembered the upheavals which had preceded
their patrons' accessions. The extent to which Spenser could make
use of Vergil's example to integrate national history into his heroic
poem is due in part to the parallels which existed between their
nations' histories and their own political as well as poetic values.

BIBLIOGRAPHY

I. Editions and Translations

Ariosto, Ludovico. _Orlando Furioso_. Trans. Barbara Reynolds. New
    York: Penguin, 1975, rpt. 1977. All quotations from _Orlando
    Furioso_ are taken from this translation without alteration.

Spenser, Edmund. _The Faerie Queene_. Ed. Thomas P. Roche, Jr., with
    the assistance of C. Patrick O'Donnell, Jr. New York: Penguin,
    1978. All quotations from _The Faerie Queene_ are taken from this
    edition, but modern practices with regard to the use of i and j,
    u and v, and italics have been followed.

Spenser, Edmund. _The Works of Edmund Spenser: A Variorum Edition_.
    Ed. Edwin Greenlaw, C. G. Osgood, F. M. Padelford, et al. 11
    volumes. Baltimore: Johns Hopkins Univ. Press, 1932-57.

Tasso, Torquato. _Jerusalem Delivered_. Trans. Joseph Tusiani.
    Rutherford, N.J.: Fairleigh Dickinson Univ. Press, 1970. All
    quotations from _Gerusalemme Liberata_ are taken from this trans-
    lation without alteration.

Vergil. _P. Vergili Maronis Aeneidos Liber Secundus_. Ed. R. G. Austin.
    Oxford: Clarendon Press, 1964, rpt. 1966.

Vergil. _P. Vergili Maronis Aeneidos Liber Sextus_. Ed. R. G. Austin.
    Oxford: Clarendon Press, 1977.

Vergil. _P. Vergili Maronis Aeneidos Liber Tertius_. Ed. R. D. Williams.
    Oxford: Clarendon Press, 1962.

Vergil. _P. Vergili Maronis Opera_. Ed. R. A. B. Mynors. Oxford:
    Clarendon Press, 1969. All quotations from the _Aeneid_ are taken
    from this edition, but modern practices with regard to the use of
    u and v have been followed.

II. Criticism of the _Aeneid_

Anderson, W. S. _The Art of the Aeneid_. Englewood Cliffs, N.J.:
    Prentice-Hall, 1969.

Bowra, C. M. _From Vergil to Milton_. London: Macmillan, 1961.

Commager, Steele, ed. _Virgil: A Collection of Critical Essays_. Engle-
    wood Cliffs, N.J.: Prentice-Hall, 1966.

177

DiCesare, Mario A. The Altar and the City: A Reading of Vergil's
    Aeneid. New York: Columbia Univ. Press, 1974.

Duckworth, George E. "Animae Dimidium Meae: Two Poets of Rome."
    Transactions and Proceedings of the American Philological Asso-
    ciation, 87 (1956), 281-316.

Duckworth, George E. Structural Patterns and Proportions in Vergil's
    Aeneid: A Study in Mathematical Composition. Ann Arbor: Univ.
    of Michigan Press, 1962.

Eden, P. T. "The Salii on the Shield of Aeneas: Aeneid 8.663-66."
    Rheinisches Museum, 116 (1973), 78-83.

Fowler, W. Warde. Aeneas at the Site of Rome: Observations on the
    Eighth Book of the Aeneid. 2nd edition. Oxford: Basil Blackwell,
    1918.

Galinsky, G. K. "The Hercules-Cacus Episode in Aeneid VIII." American
    Journal of Philology, 87 (1966), 18-51.

Getty, Robert J. "Romulus, Roma, and Augustus in the Sixth Book of
    the Aeneid." Classical Philology, 45 (1950), 1-12.

Hunt, J. William. Forms of Glory. Carbondale: Southern Illinois
    Univ. Press, 1973.

Johnson, W. R. Darkness Visible: A Study of Vergil's Aeneid.
    Berkeley: Univ. of California Press, 1976.

Lloyd, R. B. "Aeneid III: A New Approach." American Journal of
    Philology, 78 (1957), 133-51.

Lloyd, R. B. "Penatibus et Magnis Dis." American Journal of
    Philology, 77 (1956), 38-46.

MacKay, L. A. "Three Levels of Meaning in Aeneid VI." Transactions
    and Proceedings of the American Philological Association, 86
    (1955), 180-89.

McGushin, P. "Virgil and the Spirit of Endurance." American Journal
    of Philology, 85 (1964), 225-53.

McKay, A. G. "Aeneas' Landfalls in Hesperia." Greece and Rome,
    2nd series, 14 (1967), 3-11.

Norwood, Frances. "The Tripartite Eschatology of Aeneid 6." Classical
    Philology, 49 (1954), 15-26.

Otis, Brooks. "Three Problems of Aeneid 6." Transactions and Proceed-
    ings of the American Philological Association, 90 (1959), 165-79.

Otis, Brooks. "Virgil and Clio: A Consideration of Virgil's Relation to History." Phoenix, 20 (1966), 59-75.

Otis, Brooks. Virgil: A Study in Civilized Poetry. Oxford: Oxford Univ. Press, 1964.

Pöschl, Viktor. The Art of Vergil: Image and Symbol in the Aeneid. Trans. Gerda Seligson. Ann Arbor: Univ. of Michigan Press, 1962, rpt. 1970.

Putnam, Michael C. J. The Poetry of the Aeneid: Four Studies in Imaginative Unity and Design. Cambridge, Mass.: Harvard Univ. Press, 1966.

Quinn, Kenneth. Virgil's Aeneid: A Critical Description. London: Routledge and Kegan Paul, 1968.

Segal, Charles Paul. "Aeternum Per Saecula Nomen, The Golden Bough and the Tragedy of History." Arion, 4 (1965), 617-57; 5 (1966), 34-72.

Solmsen, Friedrich. "The World of the Dead in Book 6 of the Aeneid." Classical Philology, 67 (1972), 31-41.

Williams, R. D. "The Pageant of Roman Heroes--Aeneid 6.756-853." In Cicero and Virgil: Studies in Honour of Harold Hunt. Ed. J. R. C. Martyn. Amsterdam: Adolf M. Hakkert, 1972, pp. 207-17.

Williams, R. D. "The Sixth Book of the Aeneid." Greece and Rome, 2nd series, 11 (1964), 48-63.

III. Criticism of The Faerie Queene

Bennett, Josephine Waters. The Evolution of The Faerie Queene. Chicago: Chicago Univ. Press, 1942.

Berger, Harry, Jr. The Allegorical Temper: Vision and Reality in Book II of Spenser's Faerie Queene. Yale Studies in English, volume 137. New Haven: Yale Univ. Press, 1957.

Berger, Harry, Jr. "The Structure of Merlin's Chronicle in The Faerie Queene 3 (iii)." Studies in English Literature, 9 (1969), 39-51.

Bowers, Fredson. "Evidences of Revision in The Faerie Queene III.i,ii." Modern Language Notes, 60 (1945), 114-16.

Cain, Thomas H. Praise in The Faerie Queene. Lincoln: Univ. of Nebraska Press, 1978.

Candido, Joseph. "The Compositional History of Cantos ii and iii in Book III of The Faerie Queene." American Notes and Queries, 16 (1977), 50-52.

Dees, Jerome S. "Notes on Spenser's Allegorical Structures." In Spenser at Kalamazoo. Proceedings from a Special Session at the Thirteenth Conference on Medieval Studies in Kalamazoo, Michigan, 5-6 May 1978. Ed. David A. Richardson. Cleveland: Cleveland State Univ., 1978, pp. 231-37.

Elliott, John R., Jr., ed. The Prince of Poets: Essays on Edmund Spenser. New York: New York Univ. Press, 1968.

Fletcher, Angus. The Prophetic Moment: An Essay on Spenser. Chicago: Univ. of Chicago Press, 1971.

Frye, Northrop. Fables of Identity: Studies in Poetic Mythology. New York: Harcourt, Brace & World, 1963.

Galinsky, G. Karl. The Herakles Theme: The Adaptations of the Hero in Literature from Homer to the Twentieth Century. Totowa, N.J.: Rowman and Littlefield, 1972.

Gottfried, Rudolf B. "Spenser and The Historie of Cambria." Modern Language Notes, 72 (1957), 9-13.

Hamilton, A. C. "A Theological Reading of The Faerie Queene, Book II." English Literary History, 25 (1958), 155-62.

Harper, Carrie Anna. The Sources of The British Chronicle History in Spenser's Faerie Queene. Diss. Bryn Mawr College, 1908. Philadelphia: The John C. Winston Co., 1910.

Hill, R. F. "Spenser's Allegorical 'Houses.'" Modern Language Review, 65 (1970), 721-33.

Hough, Graham. The First Commentary on The Faerie Queene. Privately published, 1964.

Hughes, Merritt Y. Virgil and Spenser. University of California Publications in English, Volume 2, No. 3, pp. 263-418. Berkeley: Univ. of California Press, 1929.

Kendrick, T. D., et al. "The Elfin Chronicle." Times Literary Supplement, 47 (1948), pp. 79, 233, 275, 345, 359, and 373.

Lanham, Richard A. "The Literal Britomart." Modern Language Quarterly, 28 (1967), 426-45.

Manzalaoui, M. A. "The Struggle for the House of the Soul: Augustine and Spenser." Notes and Queries, 206 (1961), 420-22.

Miller, Lewis H., Jr. "Arthur, Maleger, and History in the Allegorical Context." University of Toronto Quarterly, 35 (1966), 176-87.

Nelson, William. The Poetry of Edmund Spenser: A Study. New York: Columbia Univ. Press, 1963.

Nohrnberg, James. The Analogy of The Faerie Queene. Princeton: Princeton Univ. Press, 1976.

O'Connell, Michael. Mirror and Veil: The Historical Dimension of Spenser's Faerie Queene. Chapel Hill: Univ. of North Carolina Press, 1977.

Roche, Thomas P., Jr. The Kindly Flame: A Study of the Third and Fourth Books of Spenser's Faerie Queene. Princeton: Princeton Univ. Press, 1964.

Thaon, Brenda. "Spenser's British and Elfin Chronicles: A Reassessment." In Spenser and the Middle Ages 1976. Proceedings from a Special Session at the Eleventh Conference on Medieval Studies in Kalamazoo, Michigan, 2-5 May 1976. Ed. David A. Richardson. Cleveland: Cleveland State Univ., 1976, pp. 95-119.

Williams, Kathleen. Spenser's Faerie Queene: The World of Glass. London: Routledge and Kegan Paul, 1966.

Additional Bibliography

I. Criticism of the Aeneid

Brenk, Frederick E. "Auorum Spes et Purpurei Flores: The Eulogy for
      Marcellus in Aeneid VI." American Journal of Philology, 107
      (1986), 218-28.

Burnell, Peter J. "Aeneas' Reaction to the Defeat of Troy."
      Greece and Rome, 2nd series, 29 (1982), 63-70.

Coleman, Robert. "The Gods in the Aeneid." Greece and Rome, 2nd
      series, 29 (1982), 143-68.

Fuqua, Charles. "Hector, Sychaeus, and Deiphobus: Three Mutilated
      Figures in Aeneid 1-6." Classical Philology, 77 (1982), 235-40.

Gotoff, Harold C. "The Difficulty of the Ascent from Avernus."
      Classical Philology, 80 (1985), 35-40.

Griffin, Jasper. Virgil. Oxford and New York: Oxford Univ. Press,
      1986.

Hardie, Philip R. Virgil's Aeneid: Cosmos and Imperium. Oxford:
      Clarendon Press, 1986.

Harrison, S. J. "Evander, Jupiter and Arcadia." Classical Quarterly,
      N.S. 34 (1984), 487-88.

Heiden, Bruce. "Laudes Herculeae: Suppressed Savagery in the Hymn to
      Hercules, Verg. A. 8.285-305." American Journal of Philology,
      108 (1987), 661-71.

Holt, Philip. "Who Understands Vergil's Prophecies?" Classical
      Journal, 77 (1982), 303-14.

Mack, Sara. Patterns of Time in Vergil. Hamden, CT: Archon, 1978.

Michels, Agnes Kirsopp. "The Insomnium of Aeneas." Classical
      Quarterly, N.S. 31 (1981), 140-46.

Oberg, Jan. "Some Interpretative Notes on Virgil's Aeneid, Book VI."
      Eranos, 85 (1987), 105-09.

Quint, David. "Painful Memories: Aeneid 3 and the Problem of the
      Past." Classical Journal, 78 (1982), 30-38.

Rose, Amy. "Vergil's Ship-Snake Simile (Aeneid 5.270-81)." Classical Journal, 78 (1982), 115-21.

Tarrant, R. J. "Aeneas and the Gates of Sleep." Classical Philology, 77 (1982), 51-55.

Tatum, James. "Allusion and Interpretation in Aeneid 6.440-76." American Journal of Philology, 105 (1984), 434-52.

Williams, Gordon. Technique and Ideas in the Aeneid. New Haven and London: Yale Univ. Press, 1983.

Woodman, Tony, and David West, eds. Poetry and Politics in the Age of Augustus. Cambridge: Cambridge Univ. Press, 1984.

Yardley, J. C. "Evander's altum lumen: Virgil Aen. 8.461-2." Eranos, 79 (1981), 147-48.

II. Criticism of The Faerie Queene

Bellamy, Elizabeth J. "The Vocative and the Vocational: The Unreadability of Elizabeth in The Faerie Queene." English Literary History, 54 (1987), 1-30.

Boehrer, Bruce Thomas. " 'Carelesse modestee': Chastity as Politics in Book 3 of The Faerie Queene." English Literary History, 55 (1988), 555-73.

Broaddus, James W. "Renaissance Psychology and Britomart's Adventures in Faerie Queene III." English Literary Renaissance, 17 (1987), 186-206.

Cheney, Patrick Gerard. " 'Secret powre unseene': Good Magic in Spenser's Legend of Britomart." Studies in Philology, 85 (1988), 1-28.

Davis, Walter R. "The Houses of Mortality in Book II of The Faerie Queene." Spenser Studies, 2 (1981), 121-40.

Deneef, A. Leigh. Spenser and the Motives of Metaphor. Durham, NC: Duke Univ. Press, 1982.

Krier, Theresa M. " 'All Suddeinly Abasht She Chaunged Hew': Abashedness in The Faerie Queene." Modern Philology, 84 (1986), 130-43.

Leslie, Michael. Spenser's 'Fierce Warres and Faithfull Loves': Martial and Chivalric Symbolism in The Faerie Queene. Cambridge: D.S. Brewer, 1983.

Lockerd, Benjamin G., Jr. The Sacred Marriage: Psychic Integration in The Faerie Queene. Lewisburg: Bucknell Univ. Press, 1987.

Miller, David Lee. The Poem's Two Bodies: The Poetics of the 1590 Faerie Queene. Princeton, NJ: Princeton Univ. Press, 1988.

Reid, Robert L. "Spenserian Psychology and the Structure of Allegory in Books 1 and 2 of The Faerie Queene." Modern Philology, 79 (1982). 359-75.

Rollinson, Philip. "Arthur, Maleger, and the Interpretation of The Faerie Queene." Spenser Studies, 7 (1986), 103-21.

Rossi, Joan Warchol. " 'Briton Moniments': Spenser's Definition of Temperance in History." English Literary Renaissance, 15 (1985), 42-58.

Wells, Robin Headlam. Spenser's Faerie Queene and the Cult of Elizabeth. London and Canberra: Croom Helm, 1983.

Wofford, Susanne Lindgren. "Gendering Allegory: Spenser's Bold Reader and the Emergence of Character in The Faerie Queene III." Criticism, 30 (1988), 1-21.

Wurtele, Douglas. "Spenser's Allegory of the Mind." The Humanities Association Review, 31 (1980), 53-66.

III. Comparative Studies

Berggren, Paula S. " 'Imitari Is Nothing': A Shakespearean Complex Word." Texas Studies in Literature and Language, 26 (1984), 94-127.

Bernard, John D., ed. Vergil at 2000: Commemorative Essays on the Poet and His Influence. New York: AMS Press, 1986.

Bono, Barbara J. Literary Transvaluation: From Vergilian Epic to Shakespearean Tragicomedy. Berkeley, Los Angeles, and London: Univ. of California Press, 1984.

Bulger, Thomas. "Britomart and Galahad." English Language Notes, 25 (1987) 10-17.

Conte, Gian Biagio. The Rhetoric of Imitation: Genre and Poetic Memory in Virgil and Other Latin Poets. Ed. Charles Segal. Ithaca and London: Cornell Univ. Press, 1986.

Gransden, K. W. Virgil's Iliad: An Essay on Epic Narrative. Cambridge: Cambridge Univ. Press, 1984.

Greene, Thomas M. The Light in Troy: Imitation and Discovery in Renaissance Poetry. New Haven and London: Yale Univ. Press, 1982.

Horowitz, Maryanne Cline, Anne J. Cruz, and Wendy A. Furman, eds. Renaissance Rereadings: Intertext and Context. Urbana and Chicago: Univ. of Illinois Press, 1988.

Kallendorf, Craig. In Praise of Aeneas: Virgil and Epideictic Rhetoric in the Early Italian Renaissance. Hanover and London: University Press of New England, 1989.

Macdonald, Ronald R. The Burial-Places of Memory: Epic Underworlds in Vergil, Dante, and Milton. Amherst: The Univ. of Massachusetts Press, 1987.

Quilligan, Maureen. Milton's Spenser: The Politics of Reading. Ithaca and London: Cornell Univ. Press, 1983.

Quint, David. Origin and Originality in Renaissance Literature: Versions of the Source. New Haven and London: Yale Univ. Press, 1983.

Rosenberg, D. M. Oaten Reeds and Trumpets: Pastoral and Epic in Virgil, Spenser, and Milton. Lewisburg: Bucknell Univ. Press, 1981.

Rostvig, Maren-Sofie. "Canto Structure in Tasso and Spenser." Spenser Studies, 1 (1980), 177-200.

Silberman, Lauren. "Spenser and Ariosto: Funny Peril and Comic Chaos." Comparative Literature Studies, 25 (1988), 23-24.

Suzuki, Mihoko. " 'Unfitly Yokt Together in One Teeme': Vergil and Ovid in Faerie Queene, III.ix." English Literary Renaissance, 17 (1987), 172-85.

Waswo, Richard. "The History that Literature Makes." New Literary History, 19 (1988), 541-64.